I0765922

SIAPO

YESTERDAY, TODAY, AND TOMORROW

MARY ANNE PECK

FA'ASAMOA ARTS

Funding for this project has been provided by the National Endowment for the Humanities (NEH) A.R.P. Act of 2021 through its local affiliate, Amerika Samoa Humanities Council, A.S.H.A.R.P. grant program.

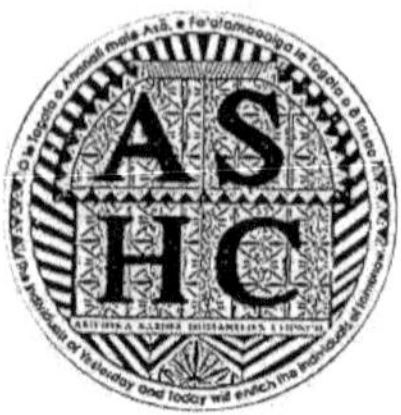

Copyright © 2025 by Folauga o le Tatau ma laga Aganu'u Fa'asamoa

All rights reserved.

No portion of this book may be reproduced in any form without written permission from the publisher or author, except as permitted by U.S. copyright law.

This publication is designed to provide accurate and authoritative information in regard to the subject matter covered. It is sold with the understanding that neither the author nor the publisher is engaged in rendering legal, investment, accounting or other professional services. While the publisher and author have used their best efforts in preparing this book, they make no representations or warranties with respect to the accuracy or completeness of the contents of this book and specifically disclaim any implied warranties of merchantability or fitness for a particular purpose. No warranty may be created or extended by sales representatives or written sales materials. The advice and strategies contained herein may not be suitable for your situation. You should consult with a professional when appropriate. Neither the publisher nor the author shall be liable for any loss of profit or any other commercial damages, including but not limited to special, incidental, consequential, personal, or other damages.

Book Cover by Su'a Uilisone Fitiao, Regina Meredith Fitiao, and Mary Anne Peck

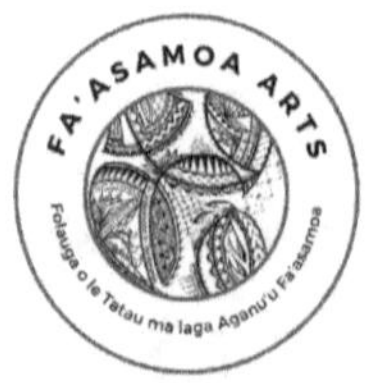

To the people of Amerika Samoa.

To the siapo makers of yesterday, today, and tomorrow.

To my students—you inspire me every day.

E teu lava e le u'a ana mea.

The u'a takes care of its own.

CONTENTS

FOREWORD

As a daughter of American Samoa and an Arts Educator for both contemporary and traditional artforms, I am pleased to say that forty years after the writing, teaching, and publishing of *Siapo: Bark Cloth Art of Samoa* by Mary J. Pritchard, the continuation of siapo making has been captured in *Siapo: Yesterday, Today, and Tomorrow* by Mary Anne Peck. When we (Su'a Uilisone & I) first met Mary Anne, she had come on island as a teacher for one of the private schools. Mary Anne's zest and interest in the Arts, especially her field of creative writing, led to many artistic and fun-filled events that would later develop into a close bond. Her desire to learn about siapo from an artistic standpoint inspired her to approach it from her area of expertise—to write about it.

This book is a testament of the legacy of siapo makers who have continued to perpetuate the art form in the modern age, who are former students of Auntie Mary J. Pritchard, and who are students of her students. Although there are some here mentioned, there are others who still need recognition. But Mary Anne's willingness to encapsulate and coordinate the wealth of knowledge about siapo and many of its unique materials and techniques became a key focal point. In addition, her writing approach to our cultural art form was for a broad audience with a desire to reach our youth, and for educators who could use it as a resource for getting started in siapo. The author has eloquently compiled information shared with her by many siapo makers who live on island today and it is fitting to say that this book confirms the ancestral art form is still being created, taught, and shared with others, both locally and in the wider diaspora. Mary Anne's attention to detail and descriptions with photographs that convey various parts of siapo making and bark cloth production in historic, artistic, and cultural viewpoints help the reader to get a better sense of the richness of siapo as an integral part of us. The author's focus is to touch those who want to understand siapo and how it is still, as it has always been, an important part of our heritage—this goal is enveloped in the pages of this book.

The siapo makers of old would be proud to see that their love for siapo has been brought into the present-day through the writing of Mary Anne Peck.

Reggie Meredith Fitiao, MFA
Siapo Maker and Professor of Art

CHAPTER ONE

E TEU LAVA E LE U'A ANA MEA

E teu lava e le u'a ana mea. **The u'a takes care of its own.**

U'a, a cloth made from the bark of the paper mulberry tree (*Broussonetia papyrifera*), has been cultivated, harvested, and utilized by Samoans for generations to create siapo, a decorated barkcloth painted with natural dyes.

The saying, "the u'a takes care of its own," is a reflection of a deeply held belief of the siapo makers of American Samoa—the belief that u'a can care for the people who make it and the people who come into contact with it. This relationship between u'a and the Samoan people goes two ways. Just as siapo makers have cared for paper mulberry trees and practiced responsible harvesting methods, so has the paper mulberry itself cared for the Samoan people by providing clothing, shelter, and a vital means of visual expression and storytelling.

In the following chapters, you will learn how siapo is made, how this art is preserved in museums, and how you can study art and art conservation to contribute to the preservation of this ancient art form. You'll also learn about the people who have spent their lives making and protecting siapo from Samoa and barkcloth from across the Pacific known as tapa.

But underneath everything you'll learn is u'a, a material that holds a spiritual power the people of the Pacific call mana. This mana exists in the siapo that is found all around the world in private homes, museums, and universities. Each piece of art carries both the mana of the siapo makers who made it and the natural materials of the Samoan islands.

In 2022, I went on a malaga with two siapo makers, the founders of Folauga o le Tatau ma laga Aganu'u Fa'asamoa (a nonprofit also known as Fa'asamoa Arts). Funded by the Amerika Samoa Humanities Council, we traveled across the United States to study siapo housed in museums and universities. That journey—the people we met, the siapo we saw, and the conversations we had—inspired this book. I hope these words serve as a method of connection between the siapo makers who have become my family and the young people of American Samoa and the wider Samoan diaspora. Every page is informed by the lived experiences of the siapo makers of yesterday, today, and tomorrow.

By reading *Siapo: Yesterday, Today, and Tomorrow*, you are taking a step in educating yourself about the indigenous artforms of Samoa, and that education helps to keep siapo alive for generations to come.

To help improve your learning, each chapter will end with a list of key terms—a combination of Samoan and English words found in that chapter. There will also be discussion questions you can use to talk about each chapter with your friends, family, or classmates.

Key Terms:

- **U'a**: The Samoan term for barkcloth made from the paper mulberry tree.

- **Siapo**: U'a that is decorated with natural dyes using Samoan ancestral patterns and motifs.

- **Art conservation**: The maintenance and preservation of works of art and their protection from future damage and deterioration.

- **Mana**: Among the people of the Pacific, mana describes a supernatural force or spiritual power that people, places, and objects can have.

- **Malaga**: The Samoan term for a journey.

Discussion Questions:

- E teu lava e le u'a ana mea. The u'a takes care of its own. What does this proverb mean to you? Do you believe that a piece of art can carry spiritual power?

- How can learning about the lives and art of siapo makers and artists help you to learn more about Samoan culture?

- If you have heard about siapo before reading this book, what do you already know? Share your knowledge with the group!

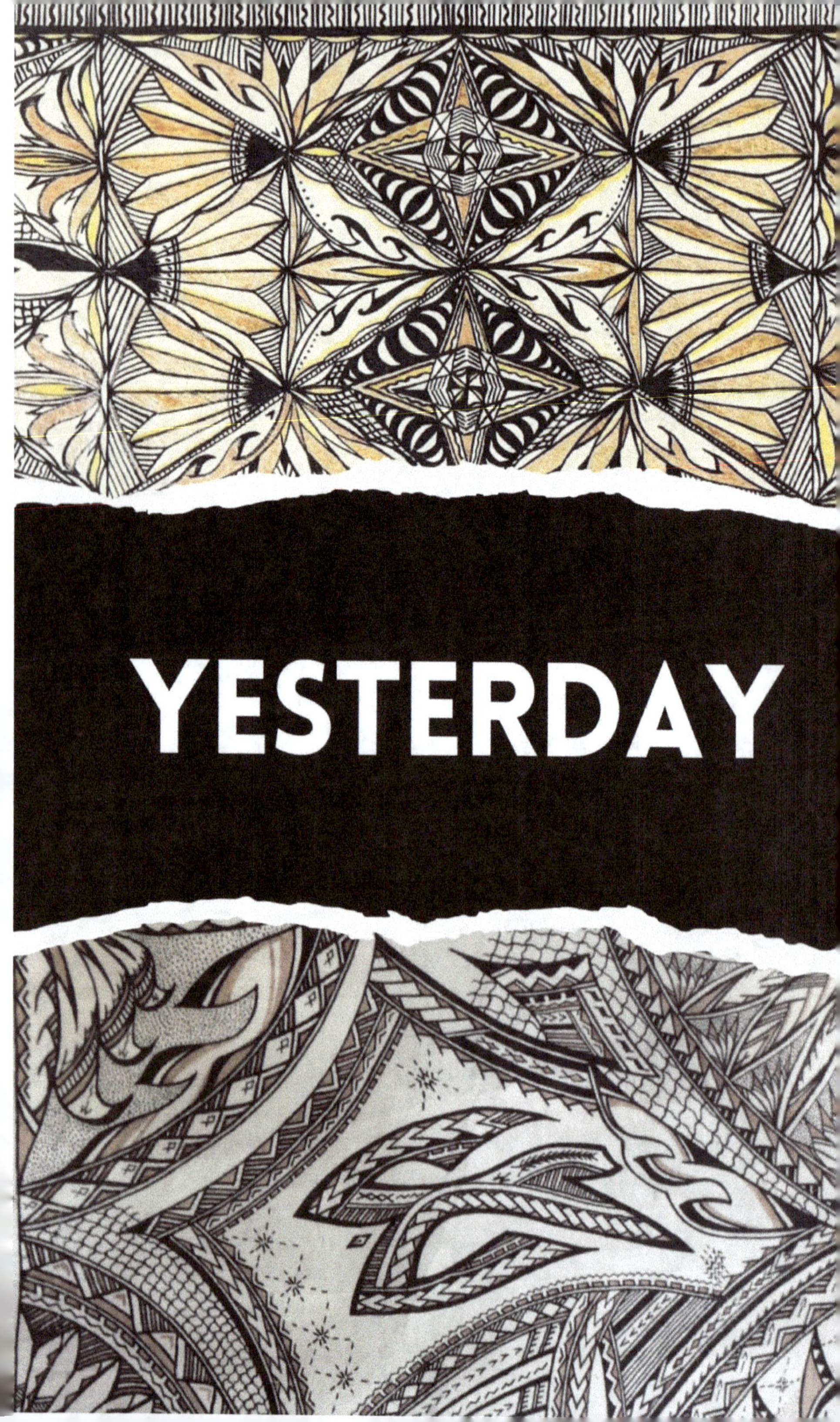

YESTERDAY

What Is Barkcloth?

Throughout history, cultures around the world have developed ways to clothe themselves, build shelter, maintain comfort, and instill tradition. Animal hides and furs, silks made by insects, grasses, plant fibers, and tree bark are used to make fabrics, which are then used to make clothes, bedding, and shelter.

In tropical environments, one type of cloth has developed over time: barkcloth, made from the bast (inner bark) of various trees, including paper mulberry, fig, and elm. Unlike many types of cloth, barkcloth is not a woven material. Threads of cotton, silk, or other fibers are not looped and knotted together to create barkcloth. Rather, barkcloth makers harvest the bast of trees and, through soaking and beating, break down the fibers of the bark to create sheets of flexible material.

Barkcloth-creation has continued for thousands of years in warm, humid climates around the world, including parts of southern Asia, central Africa, the Caribbean, and Oceania, with barkcloth makers in each location using varying materials and techniques. In the Pacific, barkcloth is known by many names, but a common, universal name for the artform is tapa.

The Barkcloth Belt: Africa, the Caribbean, Asia, and Oceania

In Africa, barkcloth creation has a history in the Democratic Republic of the Congo, Rwanda, Uganda, Tanzania, Malawi, Zambia, Ghana, and Madagascar ("The Ancient Craft of Barkcloth Across the World"). In many of these countries, barkcloth is made using the bark of the ficus tree.

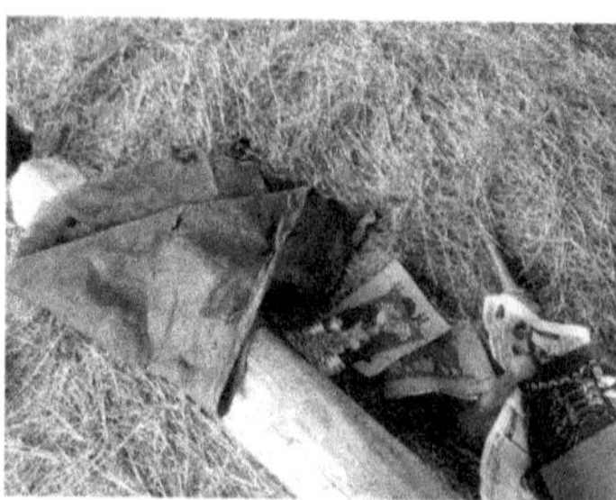

Figure 1: Barkcloth is an ancient craft of the Baganda people who live in the Buganda kingdom in southern Uganda. Oct. 29, 2021. Kyakwera. Wikimedia Commons.

Uganda has a strong tradition of barkcloth production that continues into the twenty-first century. The Baganda people of southern Uganda harvest the bark of the Mutuba tree (*Ficus natalensis*) to create their barkcloth for the people of the Buganda Kingdom (Walusimbi). The cloth is naturally a red-brown color, but may be dyed white or black to signal the status of the wearer. It is not commonly worn in day-to-day life, but is still an important part of cultural traditions for the Baganda people.

Barkcloth creation in the Caribbean was introduced when enslaved people from Ghana and the Congo began to create barkcloth in Jamaica in the 1600s. Using the plants available to them on the island, barkcloth makers developed a method for creating lacebark using the lagetto tree.

While most barkcloth around the world is made using methods of soaking, scraping, and beating the bast, lacebark is made by "teasing out the refined fibers of the lagetto bark by hand and drying the fibers in the sun," as described by National Museums Scotland.

The availability of the lagetto tree has declined, and with less material available, barkcloth creation in Jamaica reduced significantly. However, these trees can still be found on the island, and there is currently a petition to turn one grove of lagetto trees into a UNESCO world heritage site. In Jamaica, lacebark production provided ways for women enslaved by colonial powers to create clothing, earn money, and express themselves creatively (Buckridge).

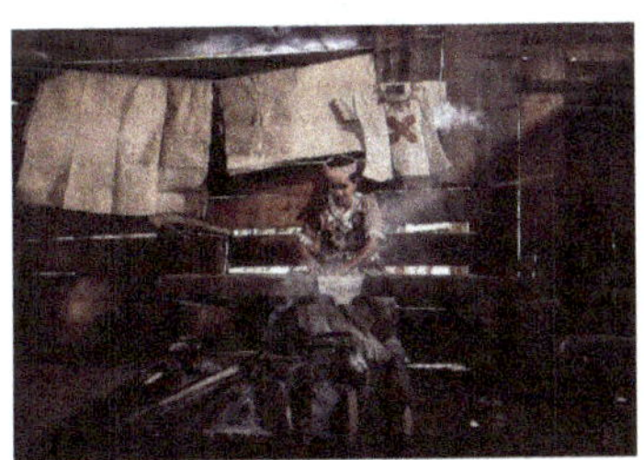

Figure 2: A barkcloth maker works to create cloth from paper mulberry and ficus trees in the central Sulawesi region of Indonesia. Sept. 9, 2019. Ganjarmustika. Wikimedia Commons.

There are various types of barkcloth made in Asia by different countries and cultural groups. For example, the Ainu people, a native population in northern Japan, creates barkcloth called attush from the inner bark of the elm tree ("Robe: Japan Ainu"). In Indonesia, the island of Sulawesi developed methods for creating brightly decorated barkcloth design. The central Sulawesi people process the bast of the paper mulberry and ficus trees and use natural dyes to create colorful fabric used for headscarves, clothing, bags, and more (Aragon).

Before international trade and colonization brought manufactured fabrics to the islands of the Pacific, many people in the region lived their lives surrounded by barkcloth.

While Samoan siapo is the main focus of this text, barkcloth art in the Pacific is not limited to Samoa. Many other people around the Pacific, such as the people of Hawai'i and the Kingdom of Tonga, make their own kinds of barkcloth art, as well. The barkcloth of the Pacific shares similarities from island to island, however, each country has specialized techniques and designs that differentiate them.

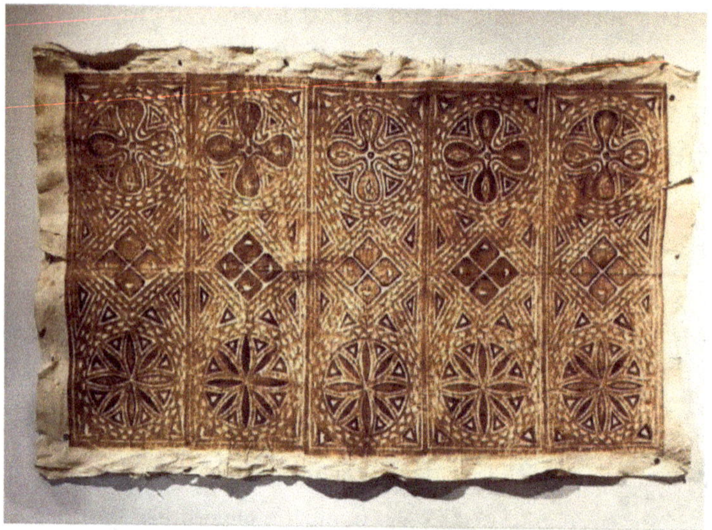

Figure 3: Siapo tasiga made from the upeti board of Lemeana'i Saiselu Tuimalealiifano Meredith. Photo from the Fa'asamoa Arts barkcloth collection.

Throughout Samoan history, siapo has served many purposes. It can be given as gifts to visitors, serve as a burial shroud, or decorate homes, to name a few of its uses. Siapo is an ancient form of Samoan art made using u'a, barkcloth created from the paper mulberry tree, and natural dyes made from plants grown in the Samoan islands. There was a sharp decline in siapo production in American Samoa after World War II due to the import of textiles from the United States, however, there is increased interest in siapo making and cultural preservation in recent years.

In Tonga, barkcloth art is called ngatu. Tongan men cultivate hiapo (paper mulberry), and Tongan women process the hiapo to create ngatu. Ngatu and siapo differ in texture, with ngatu generally being rougher to the touch. This is partly due to the speed needed to produce the amount of ngatu used in Tonga. Ngatu is one of the largest types of barkcloth currently being made in the Pacific, with some ngatu being large enough to fill a house. There are examples of ngatu that are more than 100 meters long. These tapa are commonly used for ceremonial purposes in events that involve royalty, as well as weddings and funerals (Awatea).

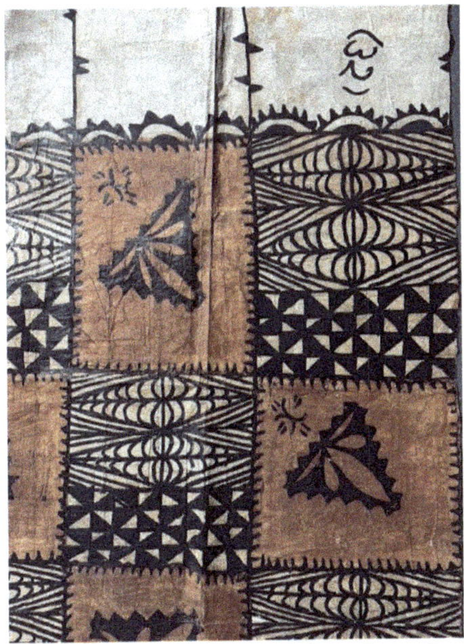

Figure 4: Tongan ngatu. Photo from the Fa'asamoa Arts barkcloth collection.

In Hawai'i, the wauke (paper mulberry tree) is harvested to create a type of barkcloth called kapa. The Hawaiian process for creating kapa diverges from the Samoan and Tongan processes, as Hawaiians soak the inner bark of the paper mulberry tree for 10 days, ferment the bark under banana leaves, and then begin beating the bark to reach its final form ("Kapa").

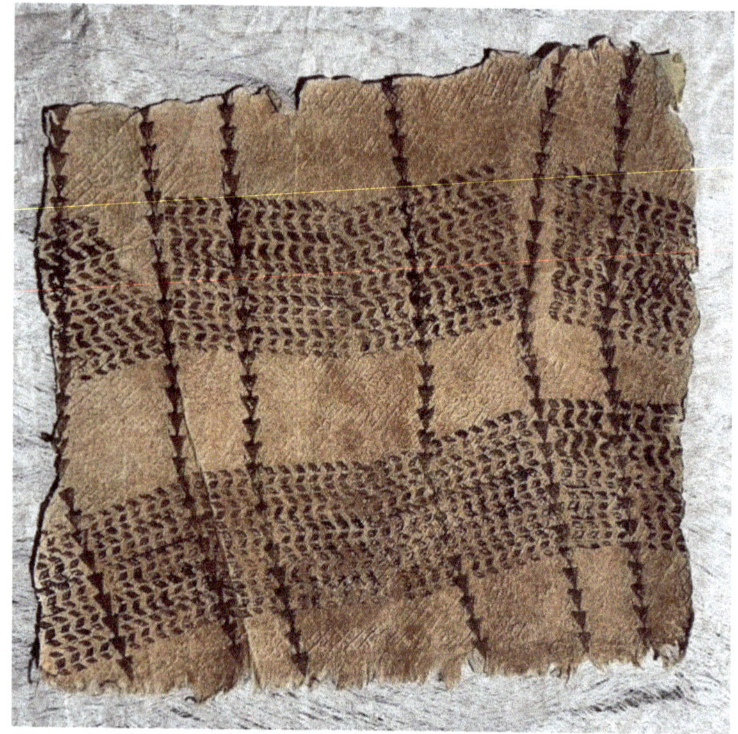

Figure 5: Hawaiian kapa by Moana Eisele. Photo from the Fa'asamoa Arts barkcloth collection.

Fijian barkcloth made from the paper mulberry tree is called masi, and is made by beating the inner bark of the paper mulberry tree (similar to processes in Samoa, Tonga, and Hawai'i). Masi makers often use stencils to create intricate patterns on the surface of the masi. Stenciled masi, known as masi kesa, is an eye-catching example of Pacific barkcloth with its geometric designs ("Masi (Tapa Cloth)").

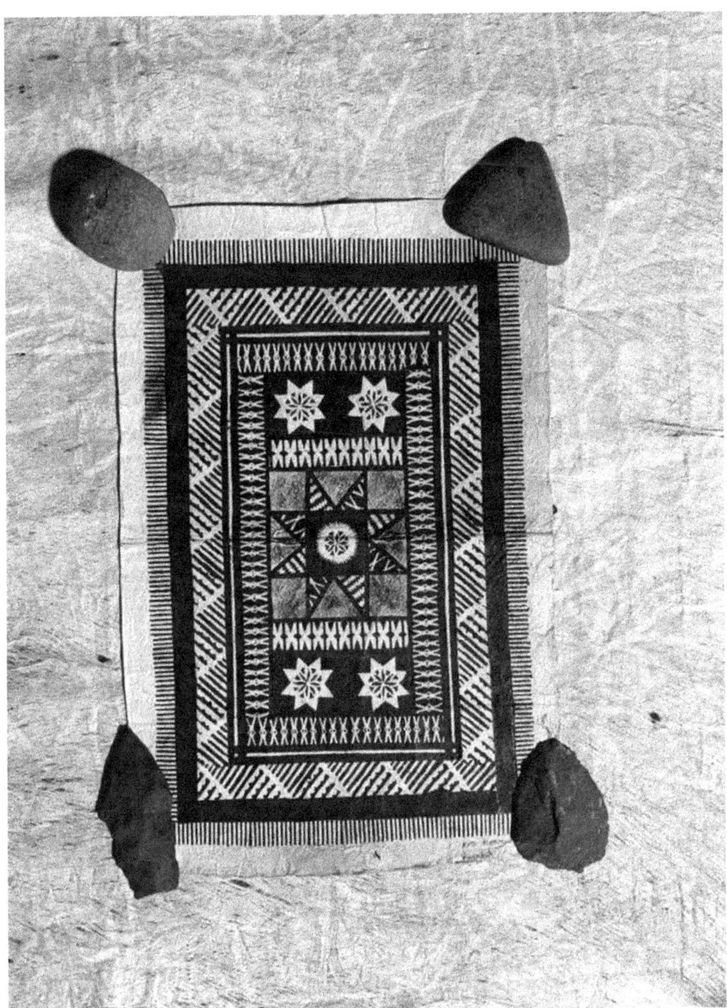

Figure 6: Fijian masi. Photo from the Fa'asamoa Arts barkcloth collection.

A Universal Name: Tapa

Throughout this book, you will see the words siapo and tapa used interchangeably. This is because, over time, tapa has become the universal name for barkcloth in the Pacific. Tapa is a word used to describe barkcloth from Samoa, Hawaii, Tonga, and any other Pacific island that makes barkcloth. It is helpful to know this word that unifies the Pacific, as well as to understand that the tapa made in each country is unique and employs different patterns, colors, techniques, and materials.

Key Terms:

- **Barkcloth**: A fabric made from the inner bark of trees. Barkcloth making involves scraping and beating the bark, then separating the fibers to create sheets of flexible cloth.

- **Bast**: A strong fiber that lays under the rough outer bark of trees. The bast is used by many cultures to create cords, matts, and fabric.

- **Lacebark**: Barkcloth made in Jamaica by teasing the fibers of the inner bark of the lagetto tree.

- **Ngatu**: Barkcloth made in the traditions of the Kingdom of Tonga.

- **Hiapo**: The paper mulberry tree and the barkcloth derived from the tree are both referred to as "hiapo" in the Tongan language.

- **Kapa**: Barkcloth made in the traditions of the Hawaiian people.

- **Masi**: Barkcloth made in the traditions of the Fijian people.

Discussion Questions:

- Which form of barkcloth discussed in this chapter interests you the most? Why?

- How does barkcloth art unify the Pacific?

Chapter Three

A Brief History of Tapa

In order to understand the origins of Samoan siapo, it is important to look at the journey that u'a has taken through the Pacific (Seelenfreund, Daniela, et al.). What Samoans call u'a has been called many names by people throughout Asia and Oceania; by researchers it is commonly referred to as the paper mulberry tree (scientific name: *Broussonetia papyrifera*). The popular name for barkcloth art in the Pacific is tapa, a word with strong connections to the Hawaiian word, kapa.

Anthropologists, historians, and botanists study the history of the paper mulberry tree and barkcloth. Understanding the origins of siapo in Samoa means looking back in time–past the original settlement of Samoa, Tonga, Fiji, and other Pacific islands to the lives of the prehistoric peoples who lived on the southern coast of Asia.

Paper Mulberry's Asian Origins

The paper mulberry tree is native to Asia, specifically southern China and Taiwan, where paper mulberry has historically been used to create currency and cloth. Researchers study the paper mulberry and artifacts found in these regions to map the movements of prehistoric communities living in this area.

One essential tool for creating barkcloth from the paper mulberry tree is a bark-beater. In Samoa, this tool is called an i'e, and it is used by siapo makers to flatten and spread the fibers of the inner bark of the paper mulberry tree. Archeologists have found versions of this tool across Oceania and southern Asia. In 2013, the oldest documented bark-beater was found in Dingmo (Bubing basin, Guangxi), China, and is estimated to be 7,900 years old. Other bark-beaters have been found throughout Hong Kong, Taiwan, and China (Li, Dawei, et al.).

Austronesian Expansion: Carrying Barkcloth Across the Ocean

The language of the indigenous people of southern Asia, specifically Taiwan, is considered the source of the Austronesian language family ("Austronesian Languages"). This language family is the largest in the world and includes languages such as Tagalog, Malay, Javanese, Fijian, Tongan, and Samoan, to name a few. The connections between these languages come from the explorations conducted by early Pacific peoples in the Austronesian-speaking group.

According to the "Out of Taiwan" theory of Austronesian expansion, groups of people left Taiwan roughly 5,000 years ago and began to settle in new places throughout the islands of Southeast Asia and

Oceania (Ko, Albert Min-Shan, et al.). As they moved, they carried plants and animals. These plants, such as taro and breadfruit, are known as commensal species or "canoe plants," meaning they were moved purposefully by the travelers as important resources to cultivate on each island.

One of these canoe plants was the paper mulberry tree. This plant was carried between islands, allowing settlers to create barkcloth in each new place.

Genetic testing of paper mulberry samples from the Pacific Islands, from New Guinea to Rapa Nui (Easter Island), led to the first plant-based genetic proof of the "Out of Taiwan" theory. Data shows that the paper mulberry of Oceania shares strong genetic connections with paper mulberry found in Taiwan (Olivares, Gabriela, et al.). The c-17 lineage of paper mulberry found in Taiwan was also found in Sulawesi, Fiji, Samoa, Tonga, Niue, the Austral Islands, the Marquesas, Pitcairn, and Rapa Nui (Matisoo-Smith).

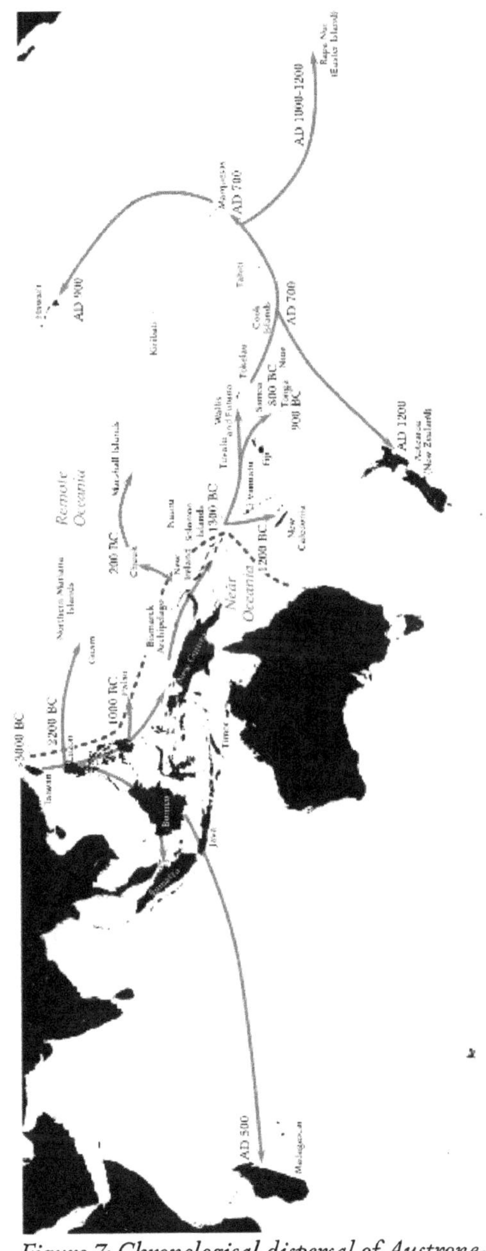

Figure 7: Chronological dispersal of Austrone-sian people across the Pacific (per Benton et al, 2012, adapted by Bellwood, 2011). Wikimedia Commons.

Barkcloth in the Samoan Islands

The oldest archeological site in the Samoan Islands is a 3,000 year old Lapita village on Upolu ("Early Samoa: History"). Lapita is the name of the cultural group of Austronesian-speakers who settled most of Melanesia and Polynesia ("Lapita Culture").

According to research conducted by a 20th century siapo maker, Mary J. Pritchard, there are not many Samoan stories or oral histories that feature siapo. However, through her conversations with several tulafale (senior orators), she learned that "Samoan tradition states that the paper mulberry plant was brought from Fiji to Fogasavai'i in the Satupa'itea district of southwest Savai'i."

These oral accounts are supported by archeological evidence that suggests that Fiji was settled 3,500 years ago ("About Fiji: History"). Shortly after the settlement of Fiji, explorers traveled east to Tonga and Samoa–bringing the paper mulberry tree with them.

Key Terms:

- **Tapa**: A "universal" term for decorated barkcloth made throughout the Pacific.

- ***Broussonetia papyrifera:*** The scientific name for paper mulberry, called u'a in Samoa.

- **Anthropologist**: An expert in anthropology, the study of humanity, ranging from the evolution of *Homo sapiens* to the societies and cultures that have developed throughout human history.

- **Historian**: An expert who studies history, the study of the events through the examination of source materials and records.

- **Botanist**: An expert in botany, a type of biology that focuses on the study of plants.

- **Prehistoric**: An adjective describing something that existed in times before written history.

- **I'e**: A wooden mallet used to sasa le u'a, or beat the bark of the paper mulberry tree to create barkcloth.

- **Austronesian language family**: A family of languages spoken in South Asia and the Central and South Pacific regions. The Austronesian language family is the largest in the world with 1,200 members, including one-fifth of the world's languages.

- **Commensal species/Canoe plants**: Plants (and some animals) that were carried by the people of the Pacific to each new island over years of exploration and settlement.

- **Lapita**: Some researchers agree that the Lapita were the original settlers of the Pacific, including Melanesia, large portions of Polynesia, and sections of Micronesia. They navigated the sea to settle the Pacific islands, arriving in western Polynesia (including Samoa) by 1000 BCE.

- **Tulafale**: A Samoan senior orator who is knowledgeable in the oral history of the Samoan islands.

Discussion Questions:

- Why is u'a (paper mulberry) studied by scientists? What can they learn from u'a?

- Why would Pacific navigators include paper mulberry with their canoe plants?

Chapter Four

A Rebirth of Siapo

Mary J. Pritchard, Siapo Maker and Educator

Mary J. Pritchard was an artist and an advocate for the rebirth of siapo in the twentieth century. She spent her life making siapo, teaching siapo at public schools, and sharing her knowledge through writing and films.

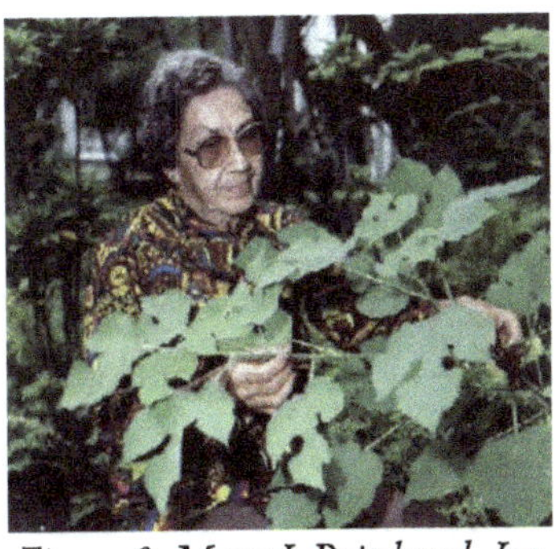

Figure 8: Mary J. Pritchard. Image provided by siapo.com.

Her book, *Siapo: Bark Cloth Art of Samoa,* has been a source of valuable information for siapo makers in the last forty years and it is through her own book that Mary Pritchard shares her knowledge for this chapter.

Mary's Early Life and Career

Mary Pritchard was born on September 17, 1905 on the island of Tutuila, raised by her mother, Felesita Fuga, and her father, Joseph Jewett. According to the artist, her childhood was filled with the "constant activity and intimate warmth typical of a large Samoan family." Her mother's aunt, Tu'u, and Tu'u's daughter, Tupito, were a stable presence in Mary's life. From an early age, they showed her the correct way to scrape the bark of the o'a tree to create siapo dyes.

"Bush trips always included older women, and it wasn't until I was much older, an adult, that I realized these women were both protecting us and educating us," Mary writes. "They were introducing us slowly and in a spirit of fun to Fa'a-Samoa, the Samoan way of life."

At the age of 18, just as she was finishing her high school education in Honolulu, Mary's father died. She was faced with a big problem—how was she going to support her mother, her brother, and her three younger sisters?

She was hired as a joiner, a carpentry-related position that was usually considered a man's job, in the Public Works Department as a sign of support for her family because of her father's career with the Navy. She was hired as "M. Jewett," and as a result she became the first woman in Samoa to be hired by the U.S. Navy, breaking barriers from a young age.

She met Ron Pritchard and they married in 1925 at the age of twenty. In 1927, she quit her job with the Public Works Department and started her own business, shipping siapo, floormats, and table mats to dealers in Honolulu. She grew her business until she had over twenty women on her payroll, working every day under the store she and her husband owned, dying fabrics and creating custom designs for customers. Her clothing items were extremely popular, resulting in so many orders that she often spent her evenings rubbing designs onto over forty yards of cloth a night.

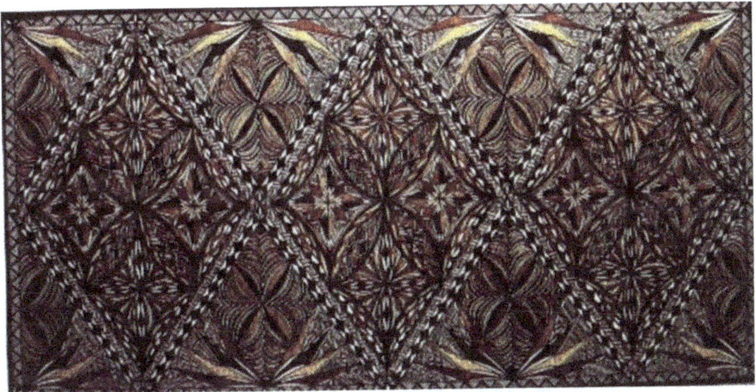

Figure 9: 1980 Siapo Mamanu, created by Mary J. Pritchard. This large mamanu is 4 by 8 feet. Image provided by siapo.com.

Entrepreneur to Artist

As her business continued to grow, so did her connection to siapo. "I found that siapo was becoming an increasingly important part of my life," Mary writes. "And it was from close to home that the most important influence was made on my artistic future."

Her husband, Ron, was from the village of Leone, and he would often visit his family there on the weekends. Sometimes, Mary would turn down the invitation to join him, saying she needed time to work at their house, but Mary writes, "Almost as soon as Ron left I wished I had gone." Sometimes she walked over four hours to get from Fagatogo to Leone. There, she would watch the siapo-making of the women in the village. She normally found herself in the home of Tui'uli Leoso, where Tui'uli's daughter-in-law, Kolone Fai'ivae Leoso, worked with other women to make siapo.

"I would be absorbed in the talk and the siapo work of the women," Mary remembers.

Kolone spent her days creating siapo designs at a lightning pace, her fingers flying over the surface of the fabric. In the quiet moments, she took the time to teach young girls in-between the many errands they ran for her.

Mary spent as much time as she could learning from Kolone, and over time, Mary's relationship with the Leone siapo makers fueled her desire to create a siapo of her own.

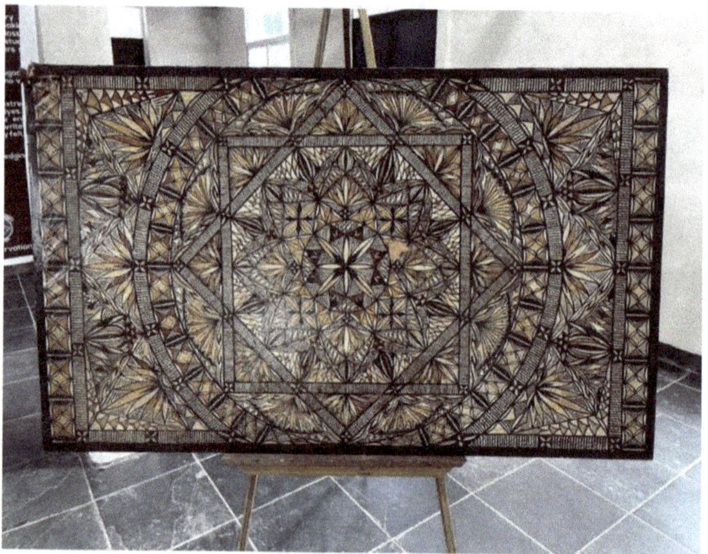

Figure 10: Siapo mamanu by Mary J. Pritchard, currently on display at Jean P. Haydon Museum.

The Savior of Siapo

Mary Pritchard has been called the savior of siapo, but from her first attempt at the artform, you never would have guessed that she would one day be famous.

She was given the materials for her first piece from the women of Leone in 1929, but she used the wrong adhesive and the entire work stuck to the counter at her store. "My first effort does not exist today, because when I tried to remove the siapo from the counter, it came up in shreds. The women in Leone laughed and joked for days about my stupidity when I joined them next," Mary remembers. Despite their laughter, the Leone siapo makers taught Mary how to properly use the adhesive and she learned from her mistake.

Her second piece was a success, but soon she realized that she had a supply problem—she had no u'a. Every woman in the Leone group had her own supply of the paper mulberry tree, but Mary had none. So she began to volunteer to help the other women with their harvesting, and in return they would give her bark so she could make her own siapo.

She grew as an artist, but with the start of WWII, almost all siapo making came to a halt. After the war, many of the women and girls who had previously made siapo never returned to the artform, and imported textiles replaced siapo in the market. Eventually, Kolone and Mary became two of the only people making siapo on the island of Tutuila.

When Kolone died in 1970, Mary was among the last siapo makers in American Samoa: "In my lifetime, the art of siapo came close to extinction," she wrote.

A New Generation of Students

In 1972, Mary began to take on students of her own, teaching them the art of siapo and sharing her knowledge with anyone who was willing to learn. She visited high schools around Tutuila, teaching siapo in art classrooms, eventually partnering with Jean P. Haydon

Museum and the American Samoa Arts Council to teach siapo in youth summer programs.

Her desire to teach siapo led her to write a book titled, *Siapo: Bark Cloth Art of Samoa*, published in 1984 by the American Samoa Council on Culture, Arts, and Humanities. This text was Mary's way of teaching siapo on a wider scale.

"I could see it as a way of reaching people beyond those I normally meet and work with in my attempt to teach the art and craft of siapo," Mary writes. "My basic purpose is to pass on something to the young people of Samoa, in a different manner through this book, but in the same spirit as those Samoan people who patiently taught and helped me."

Mary's daughters, Marylyn Pritchard Walker (1928-2005) and Adeline Pritchard Jones (1931-2005), continued to carry on the art of siapo and maintained the rich and intricate style of their mother's siapo designs. Both women engaged in their individual art-making as well as teaching siapo in various ways to perpetuate the tradition in Tutuila.

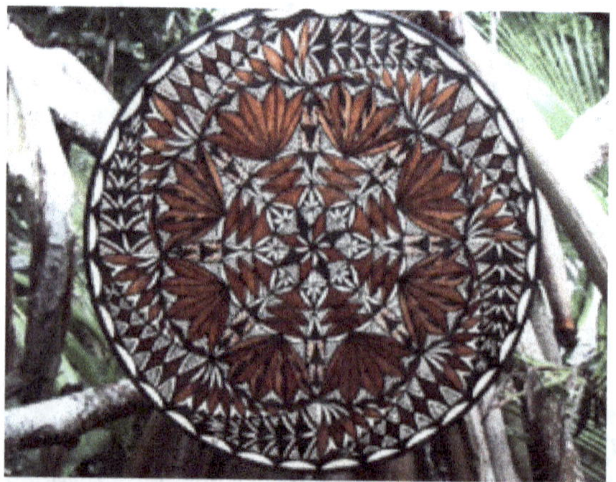

Figure 11: Siapo mamanu by Adeline Pritchard Jones. Imaged provided by siapo.com.

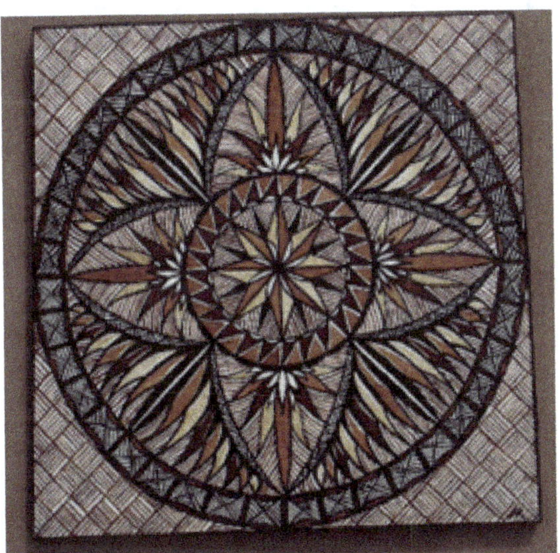

Figure 12: Siapo mamanu by Marylyn Pritchard
Walker. Image provided by siapo.com.

It is easy to see Mary's influence on her daughters' work, though Marylyn utilized larger designs with her favorite motif, ole faalaupao-go (pandanus leave), and Adeline's style involved the use of smaller motifs with less o'a brown and lama black dyes.

After Mary Pritchard's death in 1992, her students and relatives, Reggie Meredith, Uilisone Fitiao, Tupito Walker Gadalla, Maria Walker, Nick King, Wesley Sen, Rhonda Annesley, Lenita Young, Rexx Yandall, Atalina Coffin, Leslie Wood, and others, continued her work. Mary shared her knowledge with the young people around her, and the art of siapo in American Samoa saw a rebirth through her hard work and dedication.

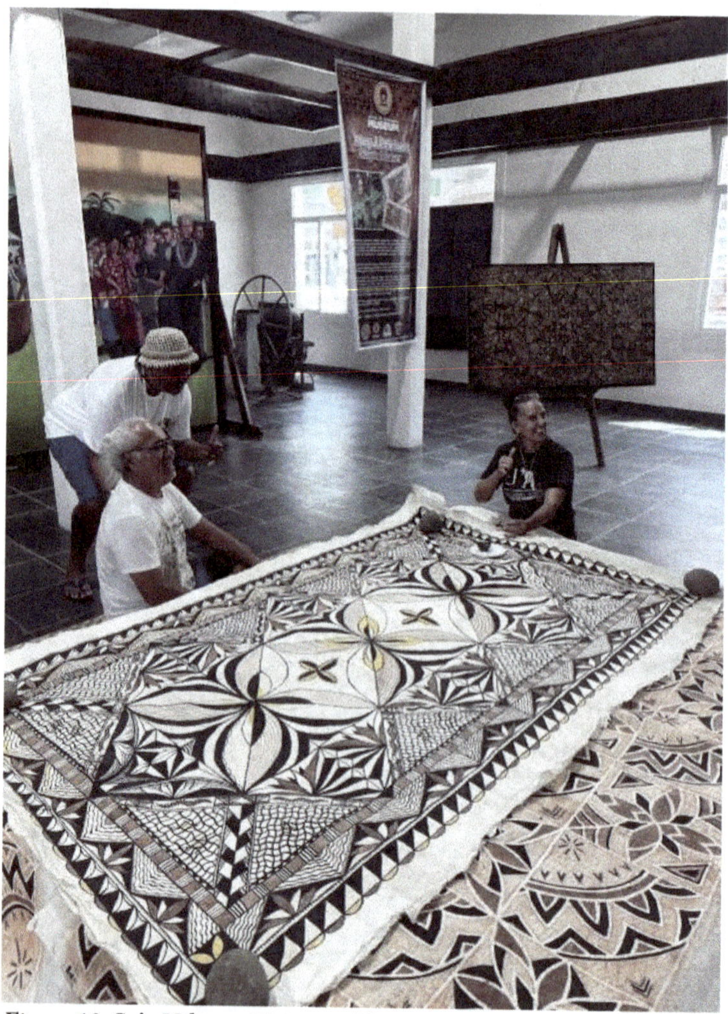

Figure 13: Su'a Uilisone Fitiao and Reggie Meredith Fitiao working on a siapo mamanu at the Jean P. Haydon Museum. Photo by Mary Anne Peck.

Key Terms:

- **Fa'asamoa**: The Samoan way of life.

Discussion Questions:

- What lesson can be learned from Mary Pritchard's mistake the first time she tried to make her own siapo? How can a mistake be a good thing?

- The women of Leone worked together to create each siapo, and siapo artists today still utilize this group method for some projects. How does working as a group add meaning to the siapo-making process?

CHAPTER FIVE

LEADING LEONE'S SIAPO MAKERS

KOLONE LEOSO AND TUI'ULI LEOSO, SIAPO MAKERS

When researching siapo makers in American Samoa, the name mentioned most often is Mary J. Pritchard. She is the most recognized siapo maker in the last hundred years from American Samoa, but even she had to learn from someone.

Leading up to the beginning of World War II, the village of Leone was an artistic center for the island of Tutuila. The siapo makers of Leone were led by Tui'uli Leoso and her daughter-in-law, Kolone Fai'ivae Leoso.

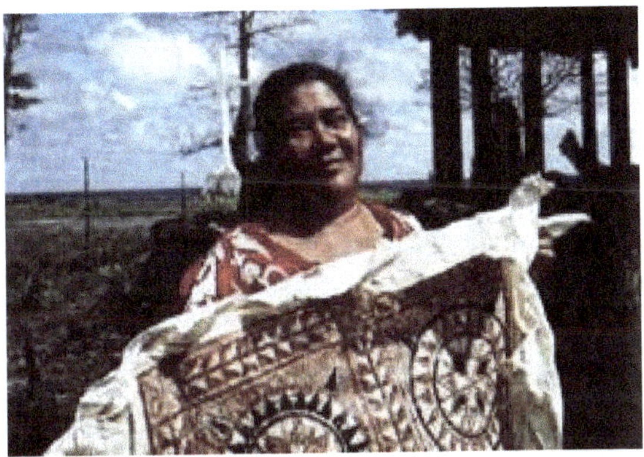

Figure 14: Kolone Leoso poses with her siapo in Leone,
American Samoa. Image provided by siapo.com.

Kolone was well known for her siapo mamanu—freehand designs. This method is prevalent in the works of art from Leone found in museums around the world, and is one of the methods Kolone taught to Mary Pritchard and others who came to her for guidance.

Kolone's Role as a Teacher

In Mary Pritchard's book, *Siapo: Bark Cloth Art of Samoa*, she writes, "[Kolone] was a stately woman, seldom speaking unnecessarily except to direct those working with her." Kolone worked constantly to create new siapo, and she "sat designing one siapo after another...Some designs were for women who would complete them for their own use, or to give as gifts or to sell."

The women of Leone began learning to make siapo from a young age. The girls of Leone spent time with Kolone and Tui'uli, completing tasks that helped the siapo makers—running errands, making food, fetching materials—and, when they were old enough, finishing designs that were started by the siapo makers.

"Some of [the siapo] were Kolone's own pieces, to be completed by young girls who would learn about siapo," Mary Pritchard writes. Everything the young girls in the village did helped them gain a deeper understanding of the importance of the artform.

There were few siapo makers in American Samoa in the years after World War II, but the work and teaching that Kolone and Tui'uli did paved the way for siapo to continue in American Samoa for generations to come.

Siapo Makers in Leone

Every morning at around nine o'clock, women walked through the village to gather at Tui'uli Leoso's house.

"Tui'uli greeted each of the women and presented each with a fa'asolo, a flower garland. There was a new one every day," Mary remembers. The women found places to sit on comfortable mats laid out in Tui'uli's fale. With u'a stretched on wooden boards and coconut shells filled with dye, the siapo makers began their work.

"Everyone in the fale had their task. That of Kolone was to design and, from time to time, correct the work," Mary writes, remembering her days spent with Kolone and Tui'uli. "That of Tui'uli was to encourage, tease and criticize the workers, direct the preparation of food for the umu and food contributed by members of the group to serve at lunch. She made sure that the needs of everyone were met."

The siapo makers worked well together, and there was always a relaxing and happy atmosphere in the fale. "Each day seemed filled with productive work, made easy by the fun."

Creating Colorful Siapo Mamanu

There are two kinds of siapo in the Samoan islands—siapo mamanu and siapo elei.

Siapo elei, also known as siapo tasiga, involves using a wood carving or other surface to rub designs onto prepared u'a. Siapo mamanu, the method historically used by the women of Leone, is a freehand method. The siapo motifs are applied by hand to the u'a with natural brushes known as paogo and natural dyes.

Siapo mamanu has been made all over the Samoan islands for generations, but at the beginning of the twentieth century, Kolone, Tui'uli, and the women of Leone began to build a reputation for their freehand skills. Mary Pritchard used her shipping connections to set up a market in Honolulu to sell the unique siapo coming from Leone, and the income helped to provide for the families of the siapo makers in the village.

Compared to other siapo makers in American Samoan history, Kolone used significantly more color in her siapo. For many siapo artists, the traditional dyes, o'a (brown) and lama (black), were most commonly used.

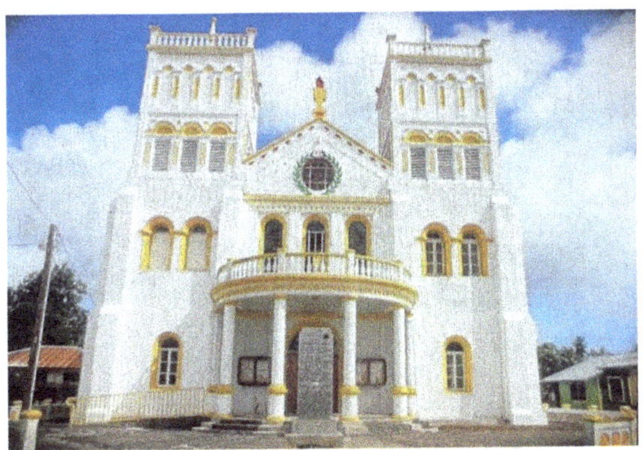

Figure 15: Siona Le Mauga Paia in Leone. Photo by Fynn Peck.

However, Kolone had a different style from the siapo makers who came before her. She and the other siapo makers of Leone were inspired by the stained glass windows of the island's churches. This inspiration caused Kolone to include heavy amounts of loa (red) and ago (yellow) dyes.

"I can remember watching her, lost in thought, staring at the church windows," Mary writes. "Turning to her blank bark cloth, she would divide the space into sections similar to those in the windows and then start to place her symbols within those spaces."

These colorful masterpieces earned Kolone a lot of attention, eventually leading to her artwork being given to the First Lady of the United States, Lady Bird Johnson.

Kolone's work led to an increased use of color in siapo over the course of the next century, and this change can be traced back to her willingness to find inspiration in her environment and take chances with her art. According to Mary Pritchard, "It was a creative break with tradition."

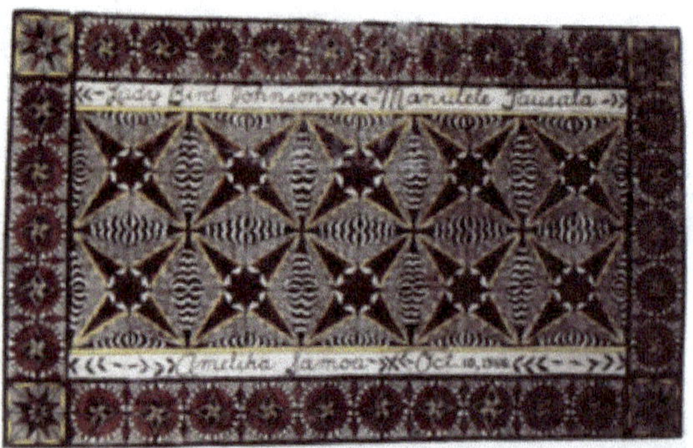

Figure 16: 1966 Siapo Mamanu. Created and presented by Kolone Leoso for Lady Bird Johnson, the First Lady of the United States. Image provided by siapo.com.

The Memory of Kolone and Tui'uli Leoso

Siapo production in American Samoa has declined over the years, but the artists of American Samoa can trace their siapo practice to Kolone and Tui'uli Leoso, who worked hard to teach the women around them about this traditional, indigenous art form.

Key Terms:

- **Siapo mamanu**: The freehand style of Samoan siapo.

- **Fale**: The Samoan term for house, an open air building that historically provided shelter for the Samoan people. Currently, fales may be used as meeting houses for families, special events, living quarters, village council meetings, and more.

- **Siapo tasiga** (also known as **"siapo elei"**): The rubbing method of Samoan siapo.

- **Paogo**: A pandanus key. Siapo makers trim the paogo to use as a natural brush for the application of dyes.

- **O'a**: The brown dye used by siapo makers, created using the *Bischofia javanica*.

- **Lama**: The black dye used by siapo makers, created using the candlenut tree, *Aleurites molucannus*.

- **Loa**: The red dye used by siapo makers, created using *Bixa orellana*.

- **Ago**: The yellow dye used by siapo makers, created using *Curcuma longa*.

Discussion Questions:

- Kolone Leoso made a difference by teaching other people and spreading her passion for art throughout her village and her island. What is something you are passionate about that you could teach to the people around you?

- Without siapo makers like Kolone and Tui'uli, siapo may have been lost in American Samoa in the years after World War II. This is just one example of how great an impact a teacher can have. Share about a time when a teacher changed your life for the better.

CHAPTER SIX

CARING FOR THE SIAPO OF YESTERDAY

MICHELE AUSTIN-DENNEHY, OBJECTS CONSERVATOR

Around the world, museums house collections of tapa, including Samoan siapo, and hire art conservators who study, preserve, and provide access to the collections.

One such museum is National Museum of Natural History Smithsonian Institution (NMNH). This museum has a large collection of barkcloth from Oceania, and Michele Austin-Dennehy is a conservator who has worked with cultural practitioners from across the Pacific to study and repair the tapa held within The Smithsonian's collections.

What Are the Goals of Art Conservation?

Through her work with museums, over many years, Michele has been a witness to important changes in the field of art conservation.

"I studied in a very scientifically-oriented conservation program in the 1980's. The focus at that time was largely on physical, tangible preservation," Michele says, speaking of her graduate education in conservation at the Winterthur/University of Delaware Graduate Program. "Over the years, there has been a shift in the goal of art conservation to include the intangible aspects of collections care leading to greater source community access and involvement."

Modern museums are prioritizing community access and involvement in different ways, including shared documentation, virtual and onsite consultations, and engaging in culturally-appropriate treatments. These practices work towards community-centered goals and, according to Michele, "That direction is essential to a holistic approach to conservation."

Documentation

Before conserving tapa or any item in museum holdings, conservators work to understand its history of manufacture and use in source communities. Documentation of life in the museum includes searching museum archives for circumstances of collection, historic images, previous exhibitions and conservation treatments. High-resolution photographs and thorough written documentation increase the level of access that people around the world have to material culture.

Once conservators have finished their documentation, information is available online. However, not every community has access to the technological tools to view digital collections, so museum professionals may send photographs and information on external drives or as hard-copies to the source communities who want to learn about the collections.

Building Connections

Throughout her career, Michele has worked directly with source communities. Many cultural practitioners and community members visit the NMNH to study their collections, guiding conservators on traditional ways of care and treatment. "As a fresh out conservator," Michele says, "I sat with a pad and pencil during consultations but learned over time that there are some cultural practices that communities don't want to share." Sometimes, visitors are there simply to spend time with the objects in the collection.

"Now the collections are very open and communities are involved in all aspects of collections care and exhibition."

Culturally-Appropriate Treatments

When conservators speak with representatives of source communities, they are often able to make adjustments in their conservation efforts to best reflect an object's cultural origin. Within The Smithsonian's tapa collection, there are many cultures represented, including Samoa, Hawai'i, Fiji, and Tonga, to name a few. While barkcloth-making is a common practice throughout the Pacific, each island nation has different practices and traditions.

"I had done some tinted paper mulberry repair on Hawaiian kapa," Michele says, remembering her time learning from Hawaiian cultural practitioners. "Over time, after talking with the Hawaiians, I took those repairs out because they were inappropriate." The Hawaiian cultural practitioners wanted minimal, clearly visible repairs. Utilizing culturally-appropriate treatments with guidance from source communities is one way Michele and other conservators are able to steward artifacts with the highest level of respect.

Treating Tapa in a Museum Setting

As a conservator with experience working with tapa, Michele has hands-on experience with the challenges museum professionals face when treating this material. One of these challenges is the size of tapa. Large tapa present difficulties with handling, storage, repair, and documentation. For example, at The Smithsonian, Michele has treated tapa so large it had to be photographed from a second story overlook.

When treating tapa in a museum, the process starts with asking questions. "It starts with trying to understand the piece," Michele says. Conservators consult archives

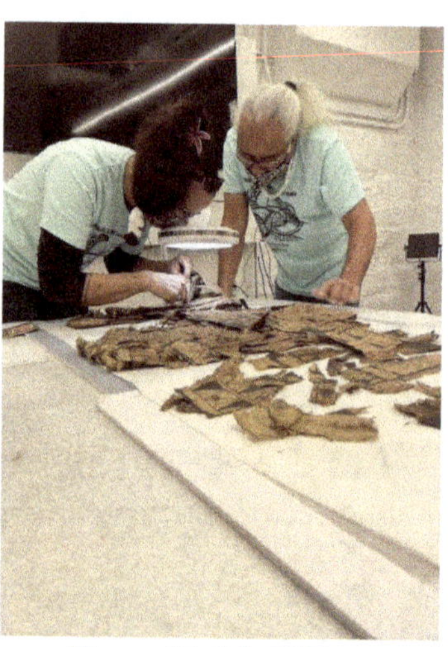

Figure 17: Su'a Uilisone and Reggie Meredith Fitiao study a heavily deteriorated siapo in the Harvard Peabody Collection. This siapo is being stored in ways that reduce the progression of future damage. Photo by Mary Anne Peck.

and study the tapa itself to learn about its journey. They ask things like:

- How was this piece collected? Who was the collector and who did they collect the piece from?

- Why are there stains, markings, or tears in the tapa? Are these caused by use or transportation? By pests?

Once a conservator has studied the tapa and learned as much as possible about its history, they may begin stabilizing torn and damaged tapa by humidification and mending. Art conservators often use wheat starch paste and Japanese mulberry tissue to mend tapa when appropriate. But sometimes, mending a tapa either isn't culturally appropriate or isn't possible due to limitations in time and funding, so tapa that is torn will be stored safely in climate-controlled spaces to prevent further deterioration.

The U.S. Exploring Expedition Tapa Project

In 2011, Dr. Adrienne L. Kaeppler, Curator of Oceanic Ethnology, and Greta Hansen, NMNH Conservator, began the U.S. Exploring (Wilkes) Expedition Tapa Project. They acquired funding that helped to bring cultural practitioners from Samoa, Fiji, Hawai'i, and Rarotonga (Cook Islands) and contracted conservators, such as Michele Austin-Dennehy, to study the tapa collections brought to the Smithsonian through the U.S. Exploring Expedition of 1838-1842.

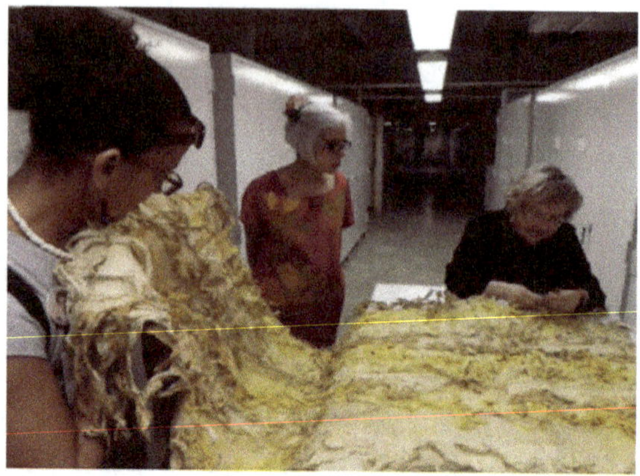

Figure 18: Dr. Adrienne L. Kaeppler, Greta Hansen, and Reggie Meredith Fitiao examine a Samoan artifact in the Smithsonian collection in 2013. Photo by Su'a Uilisone Fitiao.

The scholars involved in this project included a Samoan siapo maker, Reggie Meredith Fitiao. According to Reggie, the project included "stabilization practices, material analysis, and getting the chance to share our similarities and differences in tapa fabrication."

Reflecting on her experience with the U.S. Exploring Expedition Tapa Project, Michele says, "It was a high point for my career, that I was able to be a part of that project and that scholars from the source communities were conserving the tapa along with us. Working with siapo makers and seeing the recognition—the best part about being a conservator is seeing that homecoming and connection."

The project resulted in Reggie returning to Washington D.C. in 2014 to study siapo with Su'a Uilisone Fitiao. The two siapo makers traveled to the Smithsonian again during our research trip in 2022. The continued relationship between The Smithsonian Institution and the siapo makers of American Samoa has grown with time and led to insightful connections and conversations. According to Michele,

"It's a wonderful dialogue that you can only get with time, with sitting with someone and working things out."

Working with source communities and experts in other fields is a vital part of Michele's work. "Conservation is the process of putting a whole puzzle together and understanding these pieces and their history," Michele says. She further explains that students who aren't interested in becoming a conservator or an artist still have countless opportunities to work with siapo. The process of conservation requires people from many different specialties including scientists, botanists, historians, archivists, and cultural practitioners. "You might not want to be a conservator, but you can help out in other ways."

Key Terms:

- **Documentation**: Museum professionals keep accurate records of photographs and information about collections through documentation efforts. Through documentation, museums are able to provide the fullest possible history of each object.

- **Source communities**: The communities that created the objects currently housed in museums around the world. (Ex: Samoa is a source community for many of the tapa housed at the Field Museum of Chicago.)

- **Culturally-appropriate**: Practices, in conservation and other fields, that respect the traditions, beliefs, and preferences of source communities.

- **Cultural practitioners**: Artists and craftsmen with specific knowledge of the ancestral practices of their community.

- **Stabilization**: Practices used by museum professionals, such as conservators, with the purpose of limiting further deterioration of historical objects.

Discussion Questions:

- Art conservation has changed over the years–from a scientific focus to a collaborative process with source communities. What do you think of these changes?

- Conservators, scientists, botanists, archivists, historians, and curators—these are just some of the experts that help make art conservation possible. Which one is most interesting to you and why?

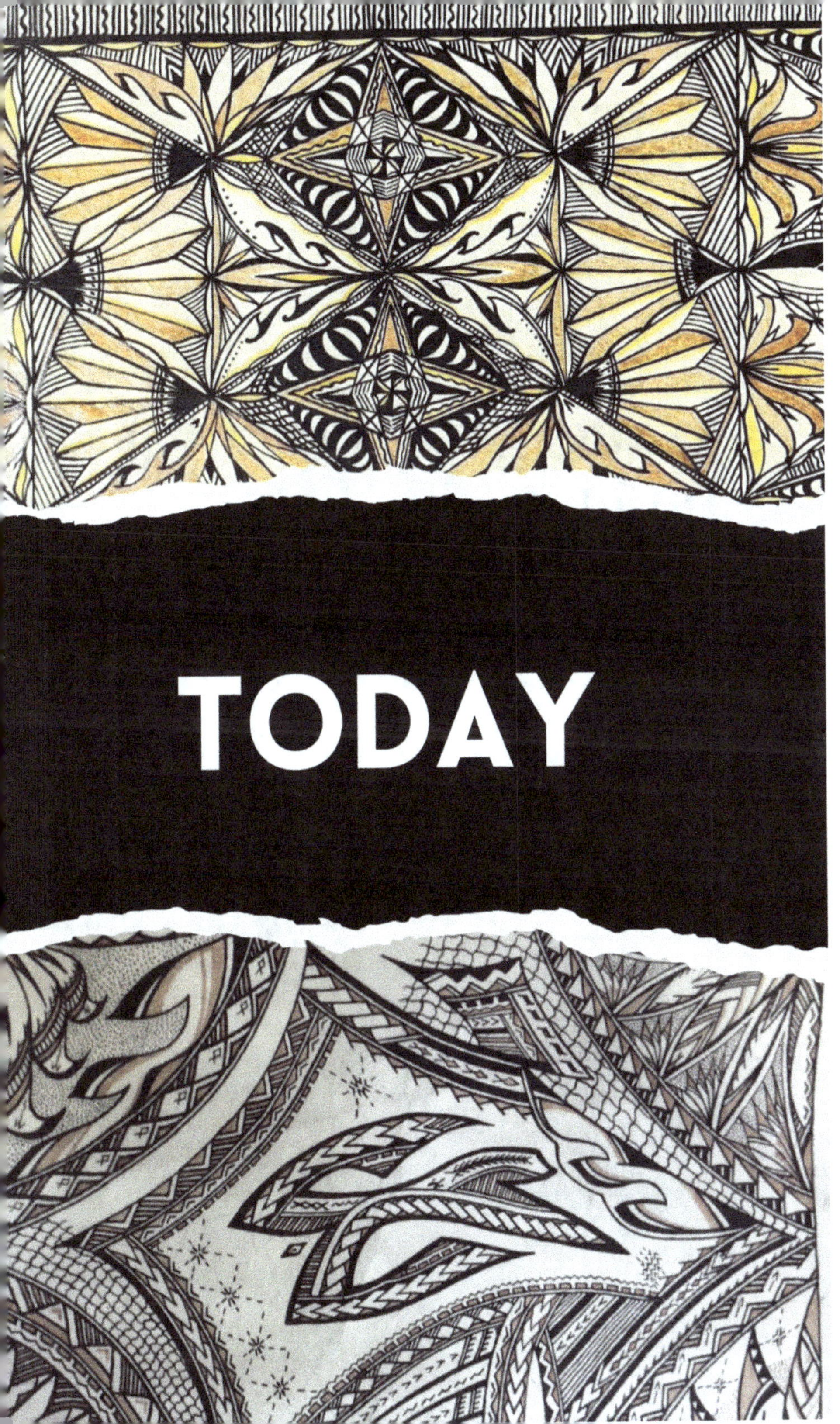
TODAY

UNDERSTANDING SIAPO AT A MATERIAL LEVEL

Siapo is made using natural materials from the Samoan islands. These plants must be nurtured and processed to form the barkcloth and dyes siapo makers use.

When looking at siapo, you may not see the months of work that went into its existence. So before you learn about siapo patterns, it's important to take time to understand the labor and materials that come before the mamanu.

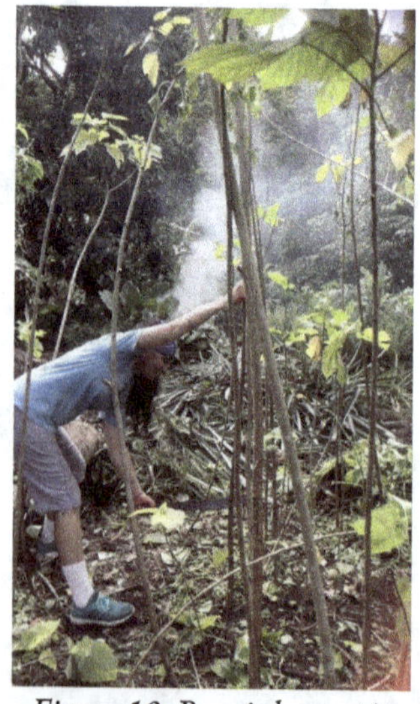

Figure 19: Reggie harvesting her patch of u'a trees in Leone. Photo by Su'a Uilisone Fitiao.

Cultivating U'a

U'a, the paper mulberry tree, grows across the Pacific and South Asia. The inner bark of these trees is an essential material for barkcloth. Historically, u'a was grown and cared for by the women in a village, led by the wife of the matai, the chief. When properly cared for, u'a can grow to be more than 16 feet tall, but siapo makers have to maintain these trees as they grow to ensure that the u'a can be used for barkcloth making.

On a weekly basis, especially early in the growing cycle, the area around the u'a must be weeded to encourage the tree's growth. Every two weeks (at least), the u'a must be checked for offshoots and new leaves. The tree will grow many offshoots and small branches as it matures, but these are trimmed by siapo makers to avoid barkcloth with holes and scars. Siapo makers work to ensure that each u'a tree grows tall with leaves only at the top.

After the u'a has been growing for roughly a year, it is matured enough to be harvested and processed.

Harvesting U'a

Traditionally, the tasks of harvesting and processing the u'a have to be completed within a few days to ensure that the bark stays hydrated throughout the process.

If a siapo maker is planning to complete the process the traditional way, they will cut the stalks of u'a the day before, covering them to prevent them from drying out. By harvesting the day before, the siapo maker is able to start processing the bark first thing the next morning.

After the stalks are cut, the siapo maker begins to strip the bark, sae u'a, from the tree. The siapo maker uses a small paring knife to make a single cut in the bark down the length of the tree. The bark is pulled from the stalk in one piece, often in a single, quick movement. Once the bark is removed from the stalk, the siapo maker peels the bast, or inner bark, from the outer bark and places it in a bowl of water to keep it moist in preparation for scraping, widening, conditioning, and beating.

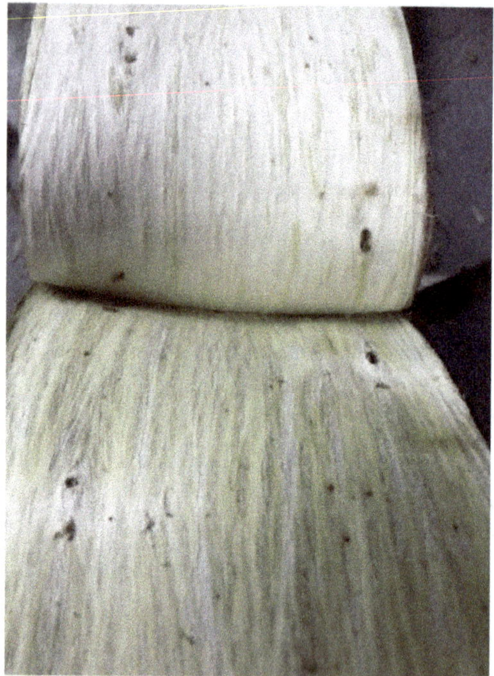

Figure 20: A glimpse of the outer bark and inner bark of the paper mulberry tree when peeled apart. Photo by Reggie Meredith Fitiao.

Creating Cloth from Bark

Once the bast of the u'a tree has been harvested, the siapo maker begins the process of turning the bark into cloth. The first step, called vavalu, is the act of scraping the u'a to remove any remaining bark and grooming the fibers to prepare for beating. The bast rests on a wooden board and is scraped with fresh water and shells in an upward motion to remove debris. The u'a tends to start widening during this step.

Once the bast is scraped, the u'a is cleaned thoroughly. After rinsing the u'a in running water, the siapo maker will fold the u'a, remove excess water, and begin to sasa le u'a, or beat the u'a. The u'a is beaten with an i'e, a wooden mallet, with smooth and grooved sides that separate the fibers of the bark to create cloth.

Every siapo maker has their own rhythm and speed as they sasa le u'a. As the siapo maker works, the folded barkcloth becomes wider and wider. Once the beating process is complete, the piece can be stretched, held down with large river rocks, and laid flat to dry.

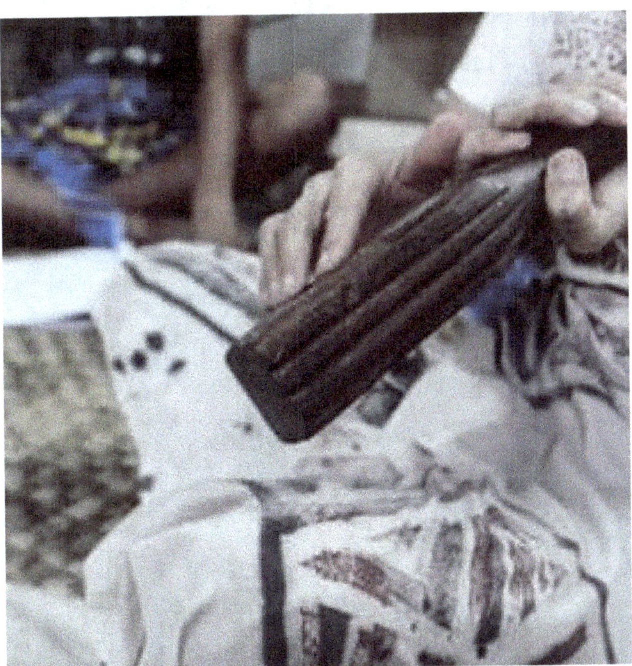

Figure 21: I'e, the beater for making barkcloth. Photo by Fynn Peck.

Preparing the Materials for Siapo Tasiga: The Upeti

Siapo tasiga, also known as siapo elei, is decorated barkcloth made using the rubbing method. In this process, siapo makers will use a carved wooden board, an upeti, and rub the carved pattern on sheets of u'a using brown dye and river rocks.

It is important to note that the upeti has changed over time in Samoan tradition. Originally, an upeti was sewn using pandanus leaves to create a raised pattern. These sewn upeti were used until the early 1900s. However, with the introduction of metal tools, the carved upeti rose to popularity, and the sewn upeti are no longer commonly used in siapo making. There are several museums and collectors around the world that store and care for sewn upeti so that historians, conservators, and cultural practitioners can study these ancestral methods.

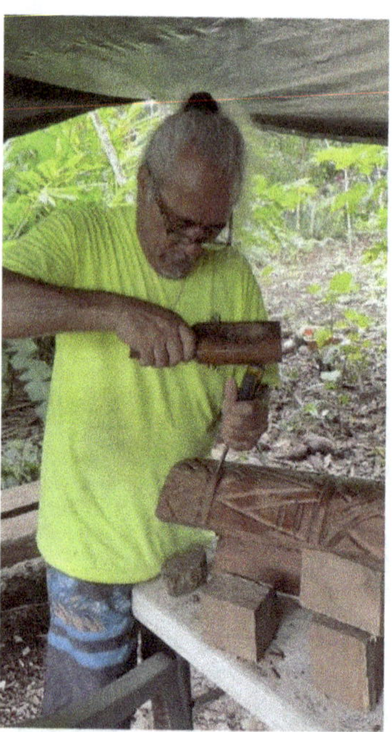

Figure 22: Su'a Uilisone Fitiao carving a design on ifilele wood using a flat chisel and mallet. Photo by Mary Anne Peck.

Carved upeti can be passed down through family lines, or shared among families in a village. In her book, Mary Pritchard writes, "Among bark cloth artists, owning a good upeti was an advantage, the more so if several boards were owned...and instead of one or two designs of our own, we had several by borrowing boards from friends and neighbors."

Sharing carved boards allows siapo makers access to a variety of designs to use in their work. And, while an upeti will continue to produce the same design, the final siapo that it makes will be entirely unique. After rubbing the design, many siapo makers will apply highlights using siapo dyes, drawing attention to specific mamanu within the rubbed pattern. The individual rubbing techniques and highlighting styles lead to countless unique, memorable siapo, all made from the same carved board.

Preparing the Materials for Siapo Mamanu: The Dyes

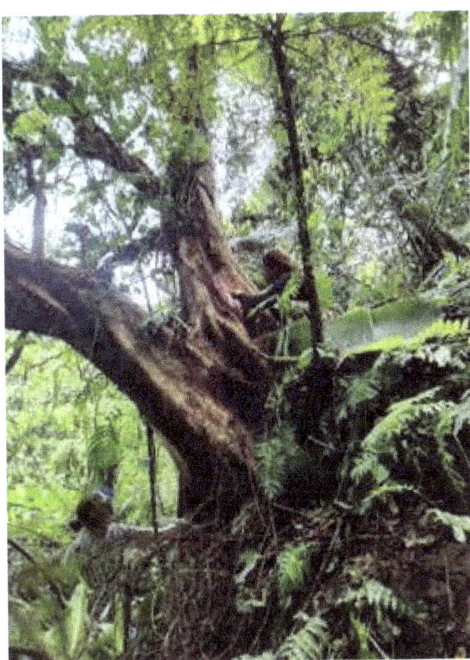

Figure 23: Reggie Meredith Fitiao and Pua Tofaeono scrape the o'a tree for the creation of siapo dyes. Photo by Tavita Tofaeono.

Siapo mamanu, the freehand style of siapo, is created by applying natural dyes to u'a using a pandanus key known as a paogo. Each dye comes from natural materials found in the Samoan islands, and is processed in different ways.

O'a

O'a, the brown dye, is at the heart of siapo. This dye can exist on its own as brown dye, but it is also used to create the lama-black dye, and can be added to the loa-red and ago-yellow dyes if a siapo maker chooses.

To begin the process of making o'a, a siapo maker has to scrape bark from the *Bishofia javanica*, the Blood Tree. Every siapo maker has a different preference. No matter the timing of the harvest, it is important for a siapo maker to care for the tree that provides this dye.

"Take what you need, and you can always come back for more," says Reggie Meredith Fitiao, a fourth-generation siapo maker and student of Mary Pritchard. "When you go to scrape the o'a, hug the tree. If your fingers can touch, the tree is too thin and young. It isn't ready to be scraped yet."

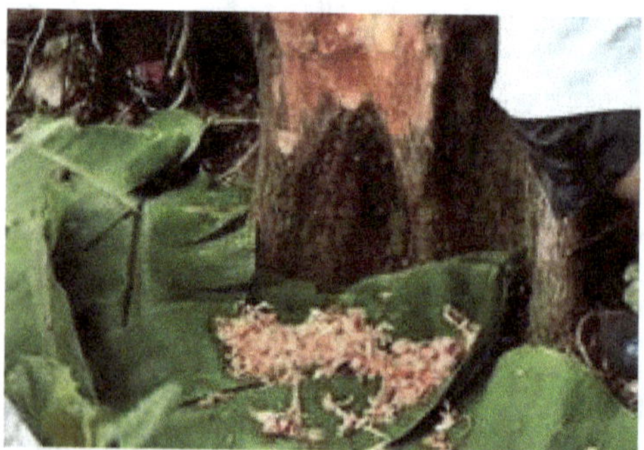

Figure 24: It is best to collect the shavings of the o'a bark for making brown dye using lau fa'i -banana leaves. Photo by Pua Tofaeono.

The siapo maker will scrape off the outer bark of the o'a tree to reveal the pink inner bark. This bark is scraped and collected until the innermost white layer is revealed. If the white bark is scraped, it can cause irreversible damage to the o'a tree. With proper harvesting methods, the tree will heal in about four years, and there are ways that siapo makers encourage healing.

"To help it heal faster and to thank the tree for providing us with the dye, we'll pick up a handful of soil and leaves and rub it on the scraped part," says Reggie.

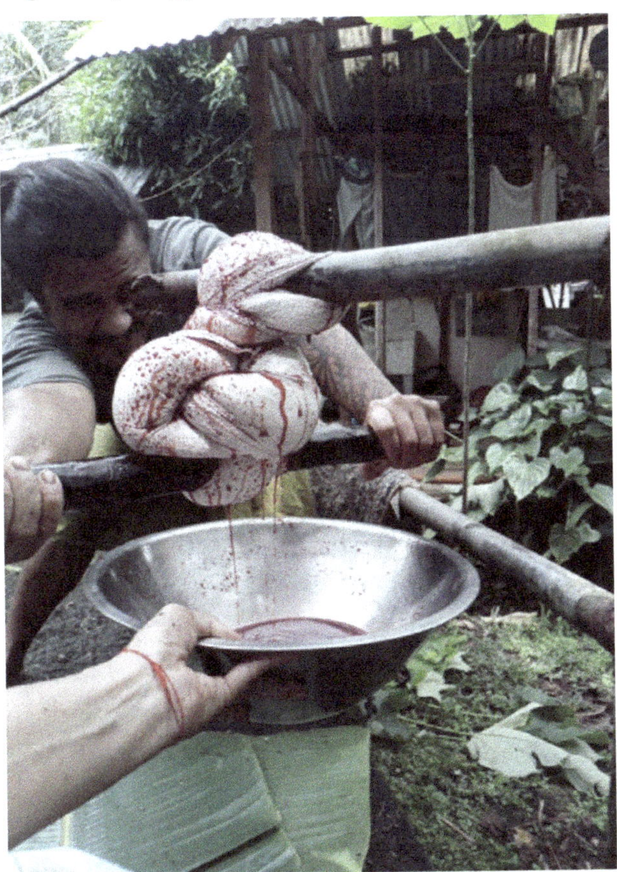

Figure 25: Mark Iulio Viliamu squeezing the o'a scraping to get the brown dye. Photo by Reggie Meredith Fitiao.

After the bark is scraped and collected, a siapo maker will squeeze the shavings to extract the juice. This liquid is carefully poured into a bottle or jar, where its uncovered for three days. If it is covered before the three days are done, the lid will burst from the pressure built up due to chemical changes in the dye.

Keeping the dye in a dark, cool place helps to prevent the dye from becoming too thick and dark to use for siapo making. Part of the natural quality of o'a brown dye is its built-in shine and ability to darken as it ages, changing the siapo with time.

Lama

Lama, black dye, is made using o'a and the soot from the candlenut tree. Traditionally, before the existence of mosquito nets and repellants, Samoans would burn candlenut in their homes to get rid of bugs.

The seeds are collected and placed in the umu, a traditional, Samoan, outdoor oven. The heat causes the seeds to crack open. A siapo maker will then skewer the inner seeds with the center of a coconut leaf to create a line of candlenut to burn. By placing a bowl or ipu lama (shell) over the burning nuts, siapo makers are able to collect the soot. When the soot is combined with the o'a dye, it creates a deep, black dye.

Loa and Ago

Loa, the red dye, is made using a seasonal plant known as the *Bixa orellana*, the Lipstick Tree. This tree can be used for lipstick, hair dye, cooking, and siapo making. The creation of this dye relies on an understanding of the natural world. Reggie says, "When you take the time to become more familiar with nature, paying attention to the seasons, like when we have palolo, breadfruit, mango, or loa, it helps us to see the resources for living that are available to us."

Due to the seasonal nature of the loa plant, the siapo maker may collect the inner pockets that hold the red seeds and freeze them until needed, allowing for the use of natural red dye all year round.

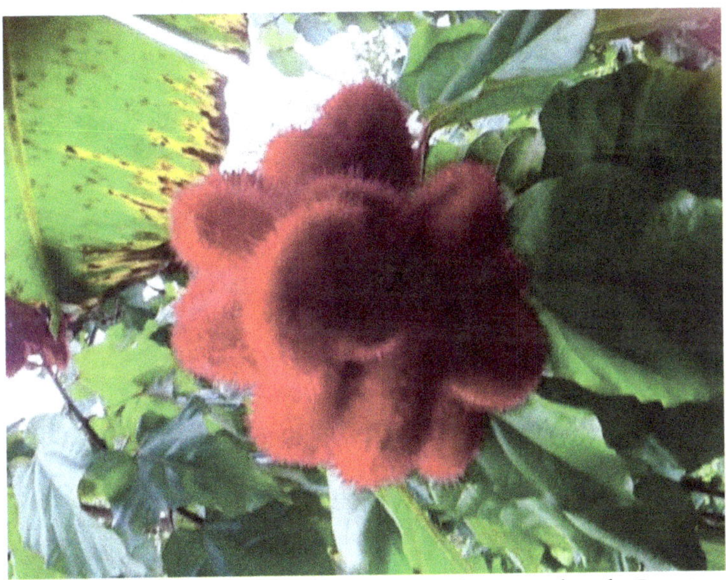

Figure 26: The loa in bloom and ready to harvest. Photo by Reggie Meredith Fitiao.

When in season, the loa dye is made by harvesting the red, prickly pods on the Lipstick Tree (*Bixa orellana*) and collecting the seeds inside. These seeds are mashed and mixed, and sometimes combined with o'a dye, to create a beautiful, rich red.

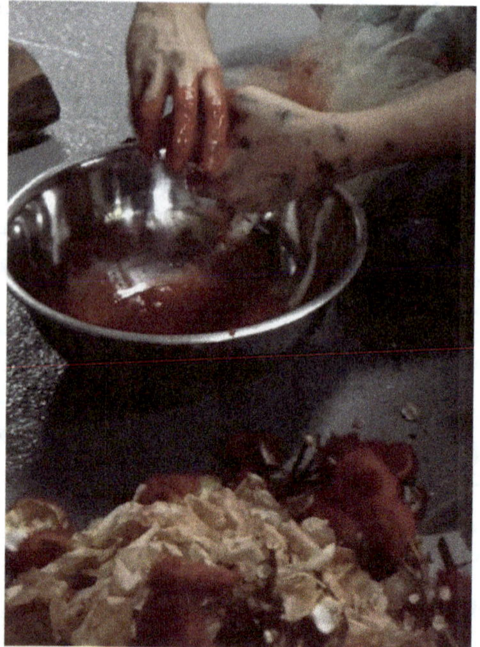

*Figure 27: Reggie extracting the loa red dye
from the seeds using a piece of barkcloth. Photo
by Su'a Uilisone Fitiao.*

The final, traditional dye for Samoan siapo is ago, the yellow dye. This dye is made by cleaning and grating turmeric (*Curcuma longa*) and squeezing it to remove the juice. The ago, like the o'a, changes over time. While the o'a darkens with age, the ago fades.

The ago is used for art, food, and healing purposes. For example, when a person receives their traditional tattoo known as la'ei, a pe'a for men or a malu for women, at the celebratory samaga, powdered lega (turmeric) mixed with coconut oil is rubbed onto the skin as a blessing and a means for healing.

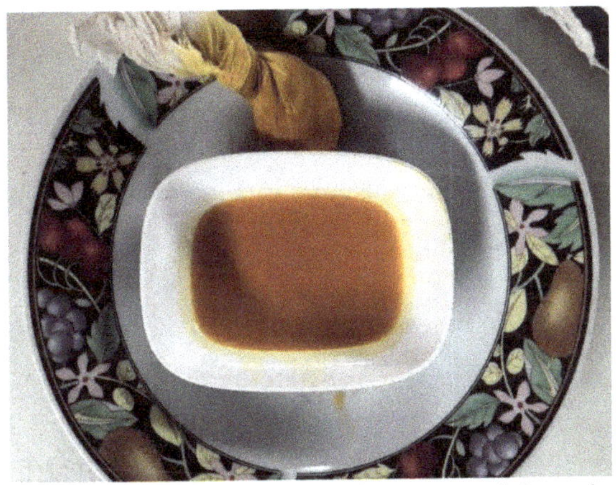

Figure 28: Ago yellow dye has been squeezed from the fresh grated turmeric root using a piece of u'a. Photo by Mary Anne Peck.

The Spirit and Power of Siapo Materials

"Look at the interconnectedness. The real strength and power of siapo has been the knowledge of our ancestors and how they maneuvered their world," Reggie says, reflecting on the materials used in siapo. These materials hold ancestral knowledge and spiritual power for siapo makers.

"Mana is a source of blessing that you inherit from your surroundings, from the earth, from the trees, from the sky, from the ocean," says Su'a Uilisone, a siapo maker and tattoo master. "Mana is power. To me, it is the most amazing blessing from nature."

In a way, siapo is a physical manifestation of this blessing. It is the combination of the gifts of nature, the knowledge of Samoan ancestors, and the dedication of the siapo maker.

Key Terms:

- **Sae u'a**: Stripping the bark from the paper mulberry tree.

- **Vavalu**: Scraping the inner bark of the paper mulberry tree to remove debris.

- **Sasa le u'a**: Beating the inner bark of the paper mulberry tree with an i'e (wooden mallet) to create barkcloth.

- **Upeti**: A carved wooden board used to create siapo tasiga. Historically, upeti have also been sewn using materials such as pandanus.

- ***Bischofia javanica***: Also known as the "blood tree," the bark of this tree is scraped and collected for the creation of o'a, the brown dye for siapo.

- **Ipu lama**: A shell used to collect the soot of a burning candlenut for the purpose of creating the lama, the black dye for siapo.

- ***Bixa orellana***: Also known as the "lipstick tree," the seeds of this tree are collected for the creation of the loa, the red dye for siapo.

- **Samaga**: A ceremonial blessing for a new pe'a or malu, the traditional tattoos of the Samoan islands.

Discussion Questions:

- If you have seen siapo before at home, in a museum, or at a market, are you surprised to learn the amount of work that it takes to prepare the materials? What did you think the process was before reading this chapter?

- Siapo makers have a strong connection with the earth and the resources that make siapo possible. What parts of nature do you strongly connect with in your life?

Mamanu: A Visual Record of Faasamoa

G athering the needed materials helps to guide a siapo maker on their creative path. Siapo makers collect these materials on an ongoing basis, creating collections of u'a and dyes for constant use.

These materials are used to create barkcloth art that includes mamanu (patterns/motifs) that have existed for generations. Before there was written language in Samoa, these mamanu acted as a way for artists to document the knowledge and daily life of Samoan people.

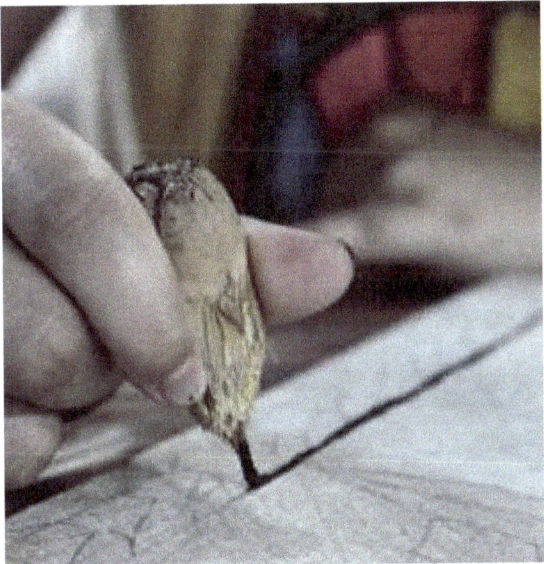

Figure 29: The paogo brush is the perfect match to painting with the natural dyes. Siapo makers trim their brushes to their own liking. Photo by Fynn Peck.

Finding Inspiration in Samoan Life

It is hard to pinpoint the exact evolution of the mamanu, but there were many guiding forces behind these patterns. The creation of the mamanu is not something that has a specific timeline, but the meanings and history of the mamanu are clear for modern siapo makers.

"Every pattern has a name, a history, and an effect on our life and our way of growing. The mamanu are like a documentary of us," Su'a Uilisone Fitiao, a tufuga ta tatau and siapo maker, says of the patterns. According to this traditional tattoo master, the mamanu are a record of Samoan life before the introduction of written language. "The mamanu teaches Samoans about ourselves, our history, and our culture."

There is a short list of patterns used in siapo (14 patterns are commonly used), but these patterns share so much more than what you may see on the surface.

"We are exercising the mamanu's importance every time we sit down to make siapo," Reggie says. "The mamanu becomes an integral part of the communication between us as siapo makers and the people who are going to see the siapo."

Fa'a ali'ao

On the surface, the fa'a ali'ao is simply a triangle. However, this pattern is a strong indicator of the connection between Samoan culture and the ocean. The triangle-shaped pattern is symbolic of the shells of ocean creatures such as the trochus mollusk, and the knowledge of fishing practices that Samoans have passed from generation to generation. This motif can be found in siapo, carving, and tatau, with each artform calling back to this ancestral knowledge.

"You can go to collect the ali'ao during the low tide," Reggie explains. "So, you have to understand high and low tides, other types of tides, and the phases of the moon." An understanding of patterns and cycles of the ocean and oceanic plants and animals has helped Samoans care for their families since ancient times.

"What does ali'ao provide? A mollusk—delicious, healthy delicacy—given to our families by the sea," Reggie says. The fa'a ali'ao motif is a reference to that knowledge.

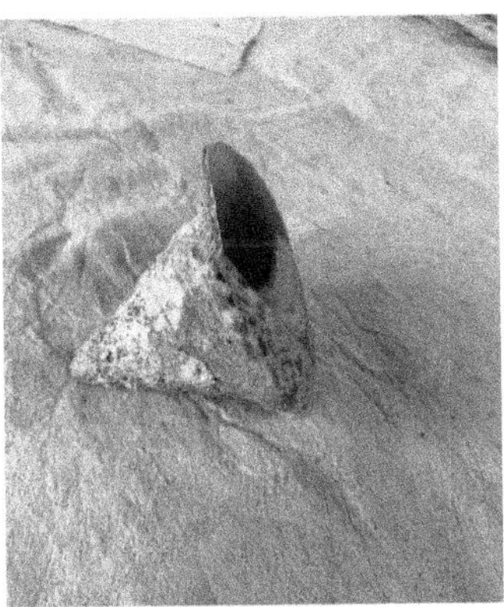

*Figure 30: A trochus shell resting
on a sheet of barkcloth. Photo by
Reggie Meredith Fitiao.*

Fa'a anufe

While the fa'a ali'ao symbolizes the ocean connection, the fa'a anufe symbolizes the connection to the earth. The fa'a anufe pattern is a simple, wavy line that represents a worm; however, siapo makers see the inclusion of the fa'a anufe as another lesson from their ancestors.

"All of the creatures in the soil are represented by the worm," Su'a Uilisone says. "The fa'a anufe pattern is about Samoan agriculture. It's about our ways of growing breadfruit and taro." This motif draws connections to the agricultural practices of Samoans throughout history.

Over the centuries, Samoan farmers have developed highly effective agricultural techniques, such as elaborate ditching systems created during prehistoric times (Shapiro). At the core of these practices is a deep understanding of the Samoan islands. Farmers look to the anufe, the worm, to learn about soil quality. When a patch of land has a high number of worms, this indicates that the soil has the right temperature, moisture, and minerals for growing healthy plants.

"The worm is a representative of the soil. It lets the farmers know where they should grow their plants," Reggie says. "This is where the mamanu becomes scientific."

Fa'a gogo

The fa'a gogo is one of the most easily recognizable mamanu: curved arches that symbolize a bird in flight. The fa'a gogo motif calls back to the navigational knowledge of ancient Samoans, a knowledge that is still used today.

"When we go out fishing, that bird brings us home. When a flock of birds join together and all go in one direction, then, from our place in the canoe, we know where home is," Uilisone says. Samoans held birds in high regard, creating three separate siapo motifs: the fa'a gogo, fa'a tuli, and fa'a vaetuli.

In a time before any GPS or navigational technology, the people of the Pacific found ways to travel thousands of miles and navigate their way between islands. The fa'a gogo pattern is one way that siapo makers worked to pass this knowledge on to future generations.

Fa'a atualoa

Each mamanu carries the knowledge of the Samoan people throughout history, but there is one mamanu that carries more than ancestral knowledge. While many of the motifs represent the land and sea, one mamanu, the fa'a atualoa, the centipede, carries ancestral suffering and resilience.

Before the introduction of bees, the atualoa (centipede) was "the only creature with a high-pain bite in Samoa," according to Uilisone. With this pain came practical knowledge, such as the stacking of rocks outside of fales to discourage the atualoa from entering. The pain of the centipede's bite also brought lessons in resilience.

The siapo makers of American Samoa view the fa'a atualoa as a symbol of hardship and suffering, and the resilience needed to overcome that suffering. The resilience and endurance of the Samoan people—past, present, and future—in the face of adversity is memorialized in siapo as a sign of respect through this motif for the world to see.

Additional Mamanu Commonly Used in Siapo

The siapo shown on the following image (Figure 31: Siapo Mamanu by Reggie Meredith Fitiao) features all 14 of the mamanu traditionally used in Samoan siapo.

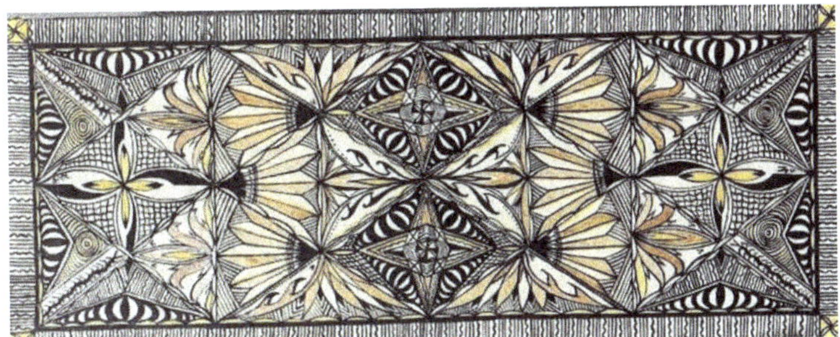

Mamanu Names:

1. Fa'a atualoa

2. Fa'a masina

3. Fa'a anufe

4. Tusili'i

5. Fa'a 'au 'upega

6. Fa'a moa fa'i / Fa'a tumoa

7. Fa'a lau paogo

8. Fa'a lau ulu

9. Fa'a 'aveau

10. Fa'a sigago

11. Fa'a vae tuli

12. Fa'a 'ali'ao

13. Fa'a gogo

14. Fa'a tuli

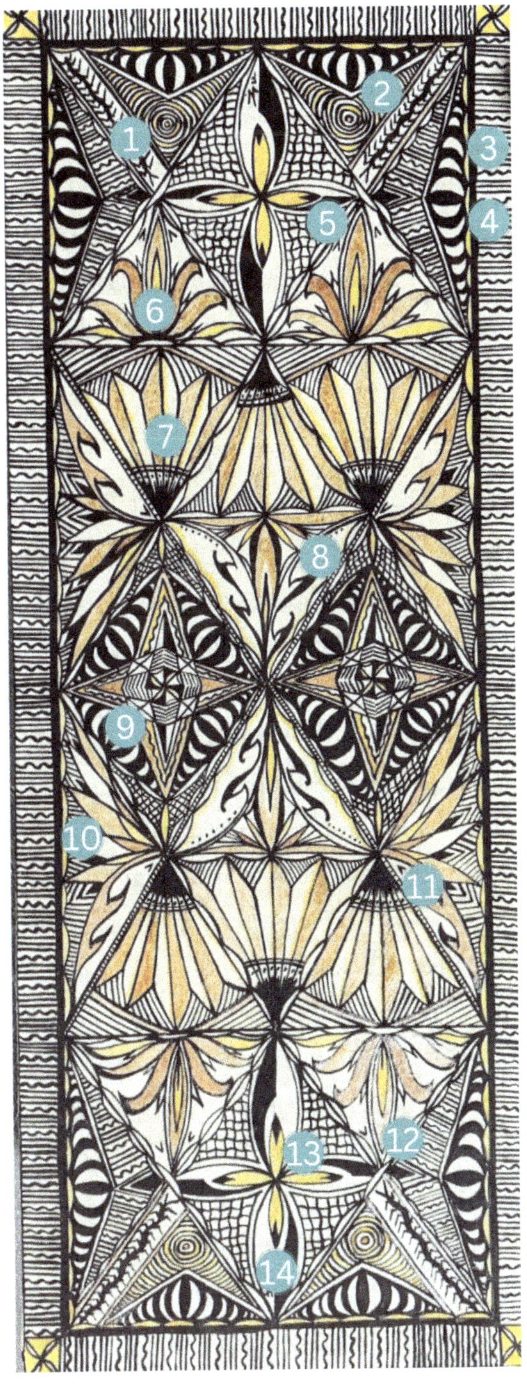

Using Mamanu with Respect

In the 21st century, siapo motifs can be found in a variety of places beyond their traditional place on barkcloth. Samoan artists, designers, and students include siapo motifs in paintings, graphic designs, fashion, and home decor, making them a common sight for those who spend time in Samoa and American Samoa. But, no matter where these motifs are used, it is important that they are used with respect and knowledge of the artform.

"There is a depth and scope that we want students to understand, going beyond the superficial beauty of the patterns," Reggie explains. "These motifs are here because, ancestrally, our people understood their world and this is the record of their understanding."

According to Su'a Uilisone, *Siapo: Yesterday, Today, and Tomorrow* provides only a small portion of the knowledge that can be learned from the mamanu: "If we explained everything that can be learned about our life and our history from the mamanu, it would take 600 books!" While reading about siapo and its cultural legacy can be an important step, there is more that can only be learned through hands-on experiences and time spent with siapo makers.

"The knowledge, it's still here, but people ignore it. Technology has distracted us so much that we are only taking from these patterns what we want for our own purposes," Reggie says. "If we give our siapo, our mamanu, the respect it deserves as an ancestral artform, it will turn around and embrace us."

Key Terms:

- **Mamanu**: The motifs and patterns used in Samoan siapo.

- **Fa'a ali'ao**: The siapo motif that represents the trochus shell and the Samoan people's connection to the ocean.

- **Fa'a anufe**: The siapo motif that represents the worm and the ancestral knowledge of the earth and agriculture.

- **Fa'a gogo**: The siapo motif that represents birds and the navigational practices of Samoans and the people of the Pacific.

- **Fa'a atualoa**: The siapo motif that represents the centipede and the resilience required to overcome hardship and pain.

Discussion Questions:

- The mamanu are one way that previous generations shared their knowledge. What is something you have learned from a previous generation through art or stories?

- The fa'a atualoa represents hardship and pain, but also the strength and resilience it takes to overcome that pain. Can you remember a time when you or a loved one was resilient in the face of hardship?

CHAPTER NINE

A STEWARD OF SIAPO

REGGIE MEREDITH FITIAO, SIAPO MAKER, PAINTER, ART EDUCATOR

Reggie Meredith Fitiao is a fourth-generation siapo maker, art professor, arts advocate, and co-founder of Fa'asamoa Arts.

Her siapo and paintings are included in collections at museums and galleries around the world, and her expertise in siapo production and siapo conservation has led to her inclusion in conservation projects, showings, presentations, articles, and workshops at the University of Glasgow, the National Museum of Natural History Smithsonian Institution, the TAPA Conference in Papeete, Tahiti, the Textile Society of America, and the Winterthur Program at the University of Delaware, among others.

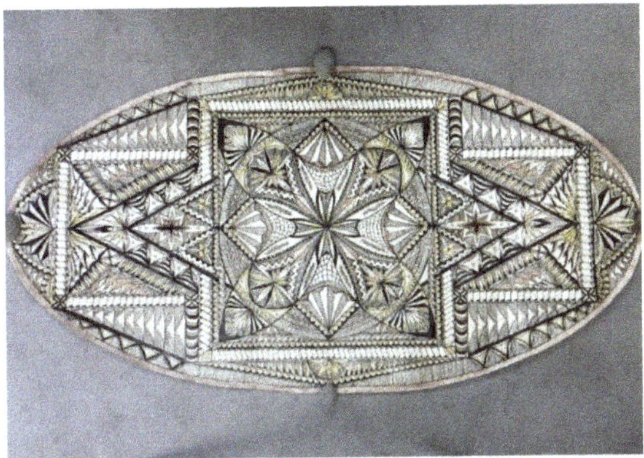

Figure 32: A siapo mamanu by Reggie Meredith Fitiao made for the conference table in the ASG Retirement Office, Centennial Building, AS. Photo and artwork by Reggie Meredith Fitiao.

Finding Siapo Through Family

Reggie was born in San Diego, California where her father, Atualevao Heinrich A. King Kong Meredith, was stationed in the Navy. He was an avid steel guitar and ukulele player, while her mother, Eleanor R. Pena Meredith, was a homemaker and seamstress. Her parents' creativity fueled Reggie and her three older siblings' lifelong interest in the arts.

Reggie knew she wanted to be an artist in the second grade, and her artistic interests grew over the years. "I was hooked on drawing Volkswagens on colorful origami paper over and over again," Reggie remembers. This innate use of repetition and pattern continued through the artist's life: "I think back on that, because in siapo there is repetition of patterns; it all started before I ever touched siapo."

Reggie's family moved home to American Samoa in the seventies, and their whole world changed. They spent time with grandparents, aunties, uncles, and cousins as they transitioned to their new life in

Leone. One place the Meredith family visited often was the village of Vaitogi, where Auntie Mary Pritchard lived in her house by the rocky coast.

"I remember the smell of the o'a dye in her house and I was always amazed by her beautiful set-up. There were tapas everywhere," Reggie says, remembering her early visits to Auntie Mary's home. Many people in American Samoa were interested in learning about siapo, and for these students, the house in Vaitogi was the place to be. "She shared siapo with anyone who wanted to learn. Even my mom learned siapo from her," Reggie says.

Reggie's early exposure to siapo involved the sights, sounds, and smells of the tapa at Mary Pritchard's home. The beautiful siapo that hung from the ceiling, the patterns, the dyes, and the tools all created a sensory experience for Reggie as a young girl, but she didn't turn her attention to siapo-making until she was a student in Auntie Mary's class at Leone High School.

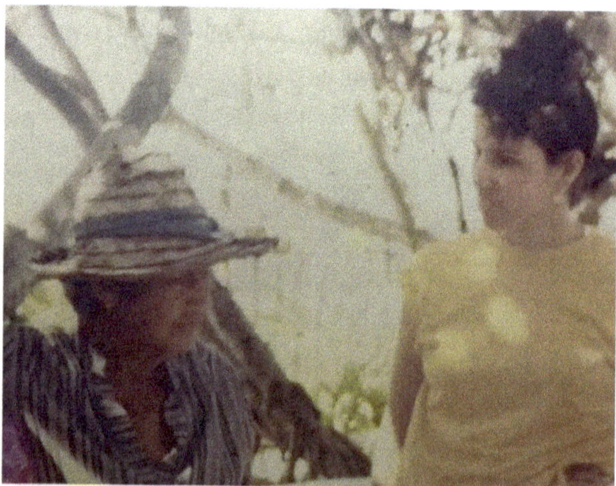

Figure 33: Auntie Mary Pritchard and Reggie spending time together in Vaitogi. Photo from the collection of Reggie Meredith Fitiao.

Becoming a Master of Fine Arts

In 1978, Reggie graduated from Leone High School and was awarded a full scholarship from the American Samoa Government. She left American Samoa to earn her bachelor's degree in Art and Art Education from Washington & Jefferson College in Pennsylvania. Upon the completion of her degree requirements, Reggie earned her certification to teach art and returned to American Samoa to teach at Samoana High School.

Soon after Reggie began her teaching career, Auntie Mary Pritchard came to her classroom to give lessons about siapo. "I wanted my students to meet her and learn from her like I did," Reggie says. "It was this wonderful, generational experience."

After teaching for two years, Reggie applied to the Master of Fine Arts (MFA) program at San Diego State University. MFA programs are considered the terminal degree for artists, meaning that the MFA is the highest level of study at the studio-level for artists, writers, musicians, and other creatives. The MFA program helped Reggie to develop her inner drive as an artist.

Among the requirements in the MFA program is a final thesis project. Reggie wrote her thesis and created a one-man art exhibition called "Visual Dynamics of Change Through Acculturation." The show was an exploration of the artist's identity and the cultural richness of her Samoan and Hispanic ethnicities. "I had to foster a true love for my afa-kasi-ness, and accept myself with the faith that my desires to inspire and connect with others through art would develop," Reggie says.

Bringing Indigenous Art Forms to ASCC

After earning her MFA, Reggie became a full-time professor at the American Samoa Community College (ASCC) in the Fine Arts Department. She realized early on that there was an obvious bias in the visual arts program in the eighties.

"The art courses all emphasized Western concepts. That's fine, but where were the courses for our Samoan art forms?" With encouragement from Samoan and Pacific Studies Director Pulefaasisina Palauni Tuiasosopo, Reggie developed a course specifically focused on Samoan art. "All of the art professors prior to me were non-Samoan. I'm sure they talked about Samoan art, but implementing a course that would enable and strengthen students in the Samoan arts was an important step," Reggie says, reflecting on her goals when creating the course. "That's when I started to be more conscious of my role as an artist and an educator and how I want to be a steward for the measina, the precious things, that mean so much to me."

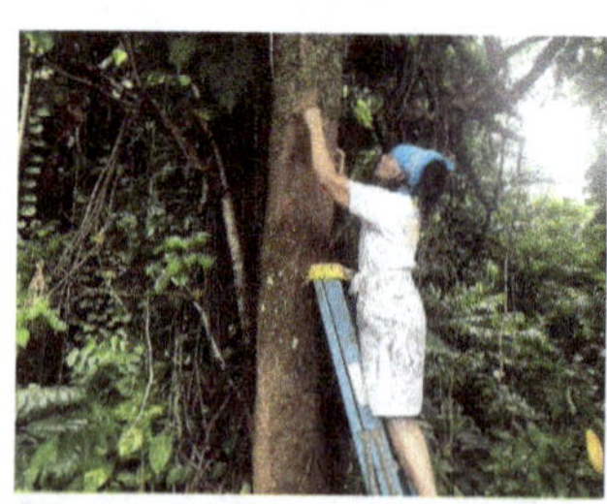

Figure 34: Reggie demonstrates how o'a trees can be scraped in various parts of the tree. Photo from the collection of Reggie Meredith Fitiao.

"It had to be so our local masters could come to share their expertise with our college students. That's how Art 161 Indigenous Art Forms began." By the time the course began, her Auntie Mary had passed, so Reggie turned to Mary's daughter, Auntie Marylyn Pritchard Walker, to provide siapo instruction for ASCC students. Masters like Marylyn, carving expert Sven Ortquist, elei master Tupu Tuiasosopo, weavers from the Territorial Administration on Aging (TAOA), and tufuga ta tatau Su'a Lesa Moli and Su'a Uilisone Fitiao came to Reggie's classroom to share their expertise with students. Reggie has continued to offer the course, incorporating lessons and input from local masters each semester.

Finding Inspiration as an Artist

Reggie's deep connection with her ancestors is a core aspect of her creative process. One of her most treasured memories is the day her great Aunt Elsie Meredith Heinrich decided to gift her with an old upeti board. "I'll remember that day forever," Reggie says. "I went over to Auntie Elsie's house next door and she took the carved board off the wall and said 'I want to give this to you. This was my mother's board, it belonged to your great-grandma Saiselu (Tuimalealiifano)'." Reggie was touched by the gesture because she'd heard stories of her great-grandmother making siapo with the women in Leone. "I know that was a defining moment for me, receiving this upeti board. It was a clear message from my ancestors that I must keep making siapo and keep going."

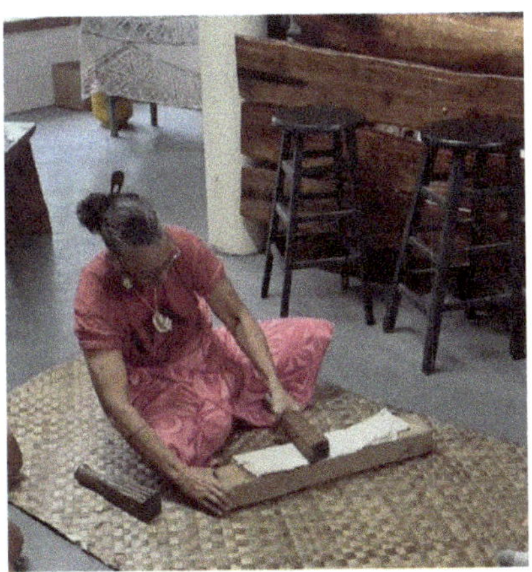

Figure 35: Reggie beats bark in her studio in Leone, American Samoa. Photo by Mary Anne Peck.

"When I work on a siapo, I think of those who came before me. I'm amazed at how they knew how to make the u'a and scrape certain trees for dyes." Reggie considers this ancestral knowledge to be incredibly valuable "because it grounds you and takes you into nature and you learn to respect the vao matua, the plush, natural forest." The artist admits that some steps in siapo-making are difficult and tiring, but these are balanced by the quiet, relaxed moments that come when painting the u'a.

When starting a new project, siapo makers like Reggie and Su'a Uilisone will spend ample time deciding what method of making is most suitable. This process can be slow, but the time is worth the outcome. According to Reggie, "Rushing siapo is not a good thing. You have to spend time with it and eventually it gives you the direction you need." With that thinking, siapo tasiga became the choice for Reggie's most recent project: a collection of 30 acoustic panels, each 3' x10' (0.9x3 meters), for the new Fale Fono Legislative Building.

A project of this size is a daunting task, but in using the siapo tasiga method, Reggie was able to add an element of communal sharing and collaboration to the project. Su'a Uilisone Fitiao carved two upeti boards for the project, and community members of all ages have visited their studio to help highlight the siapo tasiga.

"So many people have come in to share this," Reggie says. "The energy we feel when we come together to work on the siapo is difficult to describe. Everyone seems to relax and there's storytelling, singing, and laughter. It must be our ancestors surrounding us, making us feel connected and whole."

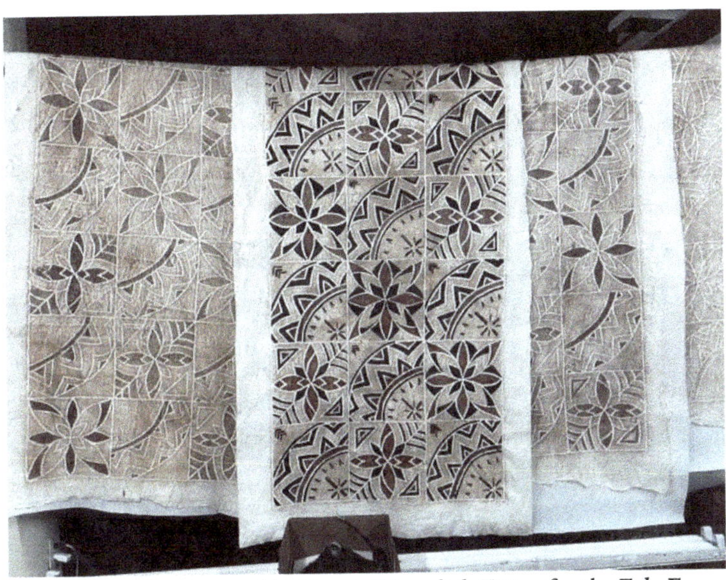

Figure 36: Tapa created by Reggie Meredith Fitiao for the Fale Fono Legislative Building at varying stages of completion. Photo by Mary Anne Peck.

Studying Art Conservation

Reggie has spent much of her career creating and teaching, but in 2013 she took on a new challenge: art conservation. Dr. Adrienne L. Kaeppler emailed Reggie and invited her to spend five weeks working on the U.S. Exploring Expedition Tapa Project with Dr. Kaeppler, Greta Hansen, Michele Austin-Dennehy, and cultural practitioners from Fiji and Rarotonga.

"In that summer of 2013, I fell in love with old tapas," Reggie says, remembering her interactions with centuries-old barkcloths at the Smithsonian. "I loved that the museum had taken such good care of our art. I loved seeing the documentation process and the conservation efforts. I had found this new love for siapo—not just in the fabrication, but in the maintenance."

This opportunity led Reggie to learn more about conservation. She began to teach her students about museum studies and she received a scholarship to attend a graduate certification course in art conservation through the University of Hawaii at Manoa (Native Hawaiian and Pacific Islander Museum Institute) and later at the University of California, Los Angeles (UCLA). The artist plans to use her knowledge of conservation to help care for the tapa in American Samoa. She says, "It's one thing to maintain our siapo on a cultural level, but it is also beneficial for us to learn museum conservation methods as well."

Working for the Future of Siapo

"In her 1974 film, Auntie Mary said, 'Today, there are just a few of us.' Here we are in 2023, and I'm saying the same thing. Today, there are just a few of us." Reggie has spent her career teaching others about the indigenous artforms of Samoa, and in 2020, Reggie and Su'a Uilisone Fitiao, decided to take their efforts to the next level.

Folauga o le Tatau ma laga Aganu'u Fa'asamoa, also known as Fa'asamoa Arts, is a nonprofit organization founded by Reggie and Uilisone to promote arts education, research, and creation in American Samoa. Through the nonprofit, they have taught siapo workshops for the island's youth and traveled across the United States to study siapo and build connections between prominent institutions and the community of American Samoa.

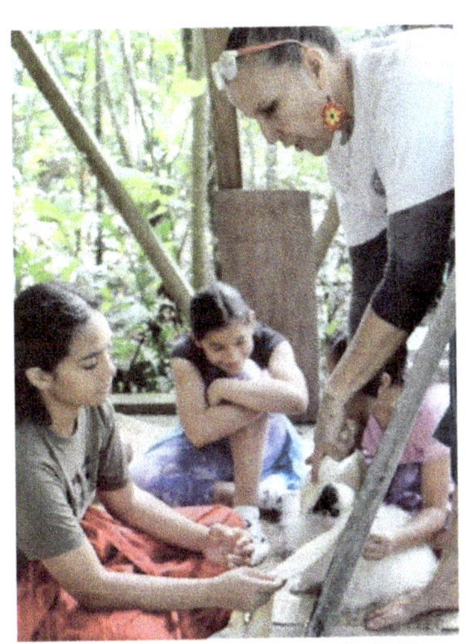

Figure 37: Reggie Meredith Fitiao instructing students during a siapo workshop sponsored by Fa'asamoa Arts and the Amerika Samoa Humanities Council. Photo by Mary Anne Peck.

After the publication of *Siapo: Yesterday, Today, and Tomorrow,* Fa'asamoa Arts has goals for future projects in Leone, where the nonprofit is based. "We want to engage more students in siapo-making. Leone was one of the central places for siapo making in the past, and I want it to return to that someday for Kolone and Tui'uli Leoso, for Auntie Mary Pritchard, for Great-grandma Saiselu and for all of those people who devoted their time," Reggie says. "Siapo is good for the soul. To touch the u'a, smell the fibers of it, and then make a work of art solely from nature –there is no comparison. We must continue making siapo for the betterment of our young people and ourselves."

Through the nonprofit, Reggie hopes to motivate others to develop deep knowledge and respect for siapo beyond the superficial use of the mamanu. She believes that there are small steps young people can take to create a better future for the art form.

"You have to start somewhere. Devote time, commit your effort, and forget about whether or not siapo will bring you income or fame. If you care for siapo, the siapo will care for you," Reggie says. "What's beautiful about siapo is that it has this indescribable ability to instill in you your cultural place, your inner strength, and your relationship to your aiga and the land on which it comes from."

Key Terms:

- **Measina**: The precious things of Samoa.

- **Master of Fine Arts**: A high-level degree that artists, writers, musicians, and actors may earn. This degree is considered the terminal degree, or highest possible degree, that one can pursue in the arts.

- **Terminal degree**: A degree that is the highest level of study in a specific field.

- **Nonprofit organization**: A business not conducted or maintained for the purpose of making a profit.

- **Aiga**: The Samoan term for family.

- **Afakasi**: To be half-Samoan and half-non-Samoan. A term used in Samoa to describe a person of mixed race.

Discussion Questions:

- Every person's identity is complex. We are a combination of the people who came before us, the cultures we inhabit, the life events we experience, and the beliefs that shape our decisions. Reggie has embraced her identity as a siapo maker *and* an artist *and* a teacher. These pieces all combine to make Reggie who she is. Try to list out some of the important parts of who you are! What are the pieces that create your identity?

- The people in our lives sculpt who we are—list some of the people who have impacted you.

Chapter Ten

A Master of Many Artforms

Su'a Uilisone Fitiao, Tufuga Ta Tatau, Siapo Maker, Woodcarver

Su'a Uilisone Fitiao is a tufuga ta tatau, siapo maker, woodcarver, and wayfinder who navigates the ocean in the way of the Samoan people.

His knowledge of indigenous Samoan artforms has led to the inclusion of his work in galleries and festivals around the world. The Smithsonian, the Field Museum, the University of Glasgow, and other institutions have welcomed his expertise and contributions to their collections.

The artist, originally from Siumu, Samoa, learned siapo from Mary Pritchard and trained as an apprentice with Su'a Lafaele Suluape to become a tufuga ta tatau, a traditional tattoo master. His role as a tufuga ta tatau has led to the creation of a style of siapo that is unique to Uilisone.

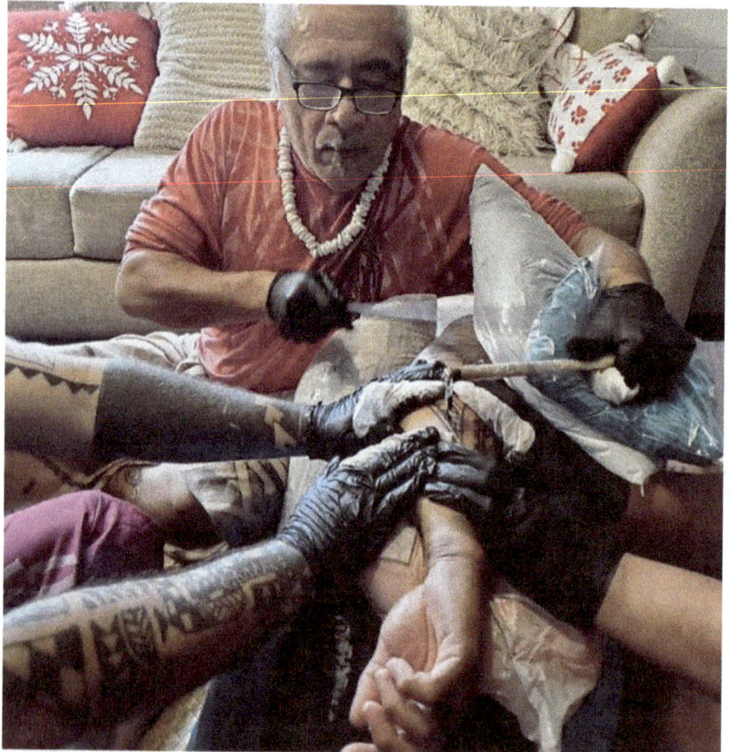

Figure 38: Su'a Uilisone working on a contemporary piece using the traditional tatau tools. Photo by Reggie Meredith Fitiao.

Falling in Love with Siapo

Art has always been an interest of Uilisone's, but before his introduction to siapo and tatau, he spent his time drawing Spiderman, Superman, and fast cars. However, when he reached high school, he met a teacher who changed his life.

"It felt natural for me to be an artist. Art was always there for me," Uilisone says. "When the old lady, Mary Pritchard, came to Fagaitua High School and I first held the paogo, I fell in love with siapo."

After high school, Uilisone kept in contact with Mary and her daughters, Marylyn and Adeline, and he began to trade artwork for siapo supplies from the Pritchards.

"I got my siapo supplies from her. I'd come to Vaitogi and give her artwork, a picture of a dolphin or turtle, and all I'd ask for in return was some u'a," Uilisone says. "I'd go home with a big bundle of u'a, and I was always so happy."

A Siapo Maker Becomes a Tufuga ta Tatau

Uilisone began to sell his art and make money as a tattoo artist while attending classes at American Samoa Community College, but his father didn't support his career choice. When Uilisone offered to help his parents with money he earned from tattooing, his father responded with suspicion.

"He was shocked; he thought I stole the money," Uilisone remembers. "But, he came to watch me tattooing one day and after that he started bragging to everyone about my art."

Uilisone's family supported his dreams as an artist, and on a trip to Samoa, they spoke with Su'a Lafaele Suluape, the head of a clan of tattoo masters, about Uilisone's work. Su'a Suluape invited him to come to Samoa, and Uilisone dropped out of college and began to work as the tufuga's apprentice.

"That's how I started the journey of tattooing, but it didn't stop me from making tapa," Uilisone says. "Every chance I got, I went to Vaitogi to get supplies from the old lady, Marylyn Pritchard Walker."

After training for seven years to become a tufuga, Uilisone felt inspired to combine siapo and tatau patterns. "I wanted to take my siapo to another level," Uilisone remembers. "So, one day I asked my master, Su'a Lafaele Suluape, if I could use the tatau patterns in the siapo and he told me I would need to ask the head of our clan, who was Su'a Paulo Suluape at the time."

In May 1999, Uilisone flew to New Zealand for the purpose of asking Su'a Paulo Suluape for his blessing to allow him to include tatau patterns in his siapo. "He told me yes, but if I do that to be sure to make it beautiful."

"I was the first person in this area to do this. I'm thankful for the blessing and authority from Su'a Paulo Suluape because my siapo making took a very important turn. To me it was what I needed."

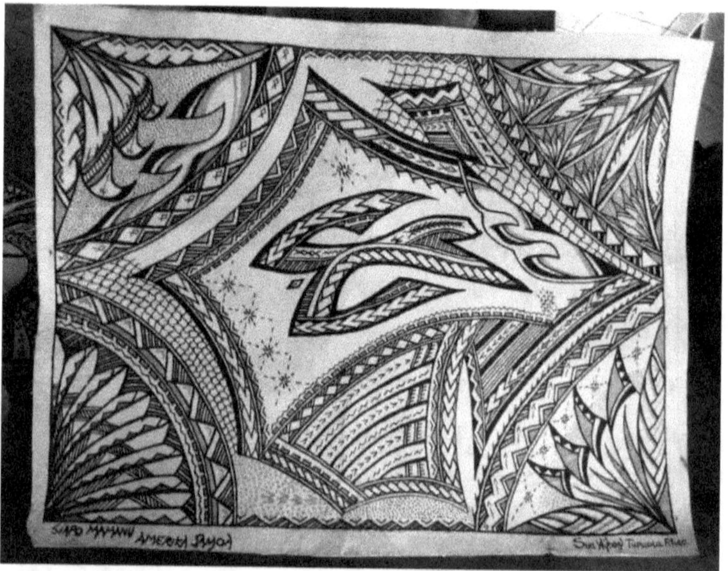

Figure 39: Siapo mamanu by Su'a Uilisone Fitiao that was made in Papeete Tahiti during the 2015 TAPA Conference. Photo by Reggie Meredith Fitiao.

Uilisone's Creative Process

Uilisone's creative process, whether he is making siapo or tattooing, is focused ultimately on acceptance. "All I have to do is listen and accept the inspiration," he says. Accepting inspiration and surrendering to the patterns helps Uilisone to create beautiful art on barkcloth and the bodies of people he tattoos.

"When I draw tapa, sometimes there are too many patterns in my brain. So I start with one line, and the pattern grows from there," Uilisone says, reflecting on the state of mind he enters when creating art. "When I tattoo a person, when the tusk hits the person's skin, then my eyes and my heart are inside the art."

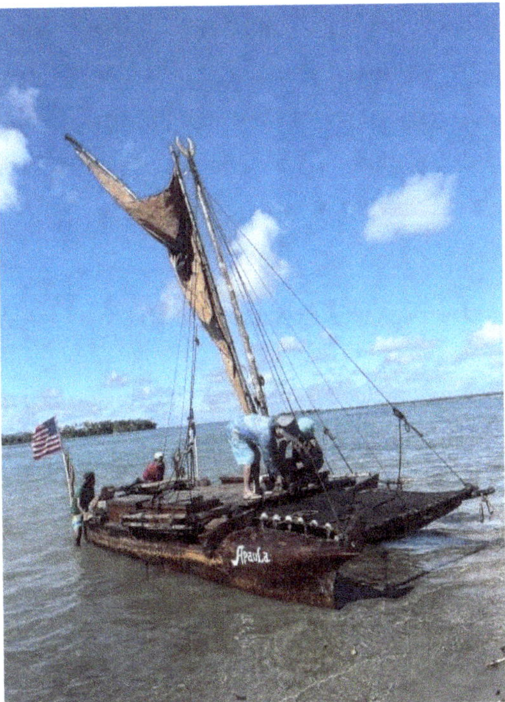

Figure 40: Apaula, a 25-foot handmade double hull wooden alia made by Su'a Uilisone Fitiao. Photo by Fynn Peck.

For the artist, the main difference between siapo and tatau is the canvas, a living canvas for tatau and a non-living canvas for siapo, but the patterns for both kinds of art are alive and hold immense power.

Much of the power that Samoan art holds for Uilisone comes from his connection with his ancestors who created these art forms. This power extends beyond his work in siapo and tatau to his work with woodcarving and navigating.

"I made a traditional boat because I believed that my ancestors would bless me and the wind would bless me. This is how our ancestors traveled," Uilisone says, remembering the process of building his boat, *Apaula*. Each of the siapo and tatau patterns helps him to connect with his ancestors in a similar way. "In the past, the wives of high chiefs, the old ladies, they made decisions about the siapo patterns and they created a history of our island with pictures."

This act of carrying ancient Samoan art forms forward is the motivation that drives Uilisone's creativity and his interactions with the young people of American Samoa.

Teaching the Next Generation of Samoan Artists

"Technology is moving like crazy, and art is being pushed back. Siapo will be gone if none of our young people pick it up and carry it on," Uilisone says when asked about the future of siapo. "I'm praying that there will be more siapo makers in the future than there are now. It all depends on the kids."

For Uilisone, teaching young people is a way to honor his teachers and the knowledge they shared with him. He has spent several years training his apprentice, Mark Iulio Viliamu, to someday become a tufuga. Through the nonprofit Fa'asamoa Arts, Uilisone and Reggie

Fitiao have been able to lead siapo workshops with young people, and plan to host more of these workshops in the future.

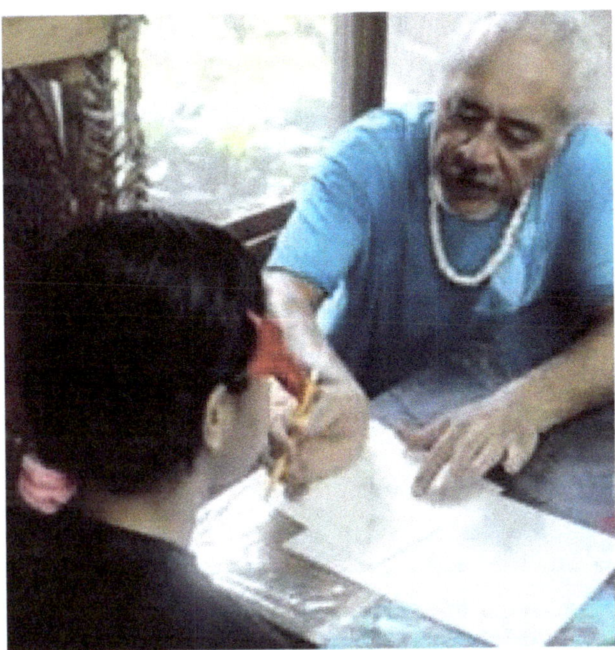

Figure 41: Discussing pattern and design possibilities with one of the students at the siapo workshops hosted by Fa'asamoa Arts (funded by Amerika Samoa Humanities Council). Photo by Fynn Peck.

"We want the young ones to know how valuable siapo is to our culture. We want apprentices. We want to know that when we die there is someone still making siapo in American Samoa." Uilisone and Reggie teach any students who are willing to learn, and Uilisone has advice to share with readers of *Siapo: Yesterday, Today, and Tomorrow*:

"My advice to students is to hold on to what you can learn about siapo and when you get the chance to spend time with siapo makers, don't stop. We won't push you away. We'll accept you with open arms."

Key Terms:

- **Tufuga ta tatau**: A master of the ancestral artform of Samoan tattoo. A tufuga must train for several years under the guidance of a master to earn their title.

- **Wayfinding**: A practice of navigation and sailing in the tradition of the Samoan people.

- **Apprentice**: One who is learning by practical experience under skilled workers of a trade, art, or calling.

Discussion Questions:

- Su'a Uilisone took extra steps to receive a blessing from his teacher before using tatau motifs in his siapo. These extra steps are just one way that he shows respect for the masters who came before him. What are some ways that you can show respect and acknowledge the people who came before you?

- Based on what you read in Su'a Uilisone's chapter—what do you think the differences are between tatau motifs and siapo motifs?

Chapter Eleven

Bringing Siapo to New Materials

Nicholas F. King Jr., Siapo Maker and Artist

Nicholas F. King Jr. has spent his life applying siapo techniques and patterns in alternative ways. His work includes items such as straw hats, baseball caps, visors, clay flower pots, water flasks, and coffee cups decorated with siapo motifs and designs commissioned by patrons and local businesses in American Samoa.

Nick has been a contributing artist on various local projects, including the mural project in Utulei and a series of siapo created for the new legislative building, the Fono of American Samoa, in 2023. His style is influenced by the artists who have taught and inspired him, including Grandmother Saitutuila Toosa'vili Taifane Brown, Nicholas and Aga King, Mary Pritchard, Adeline Huff, Rhonda Annesley, Sven Ortquist, Sau Ueligitone, and Marylyn Walker.

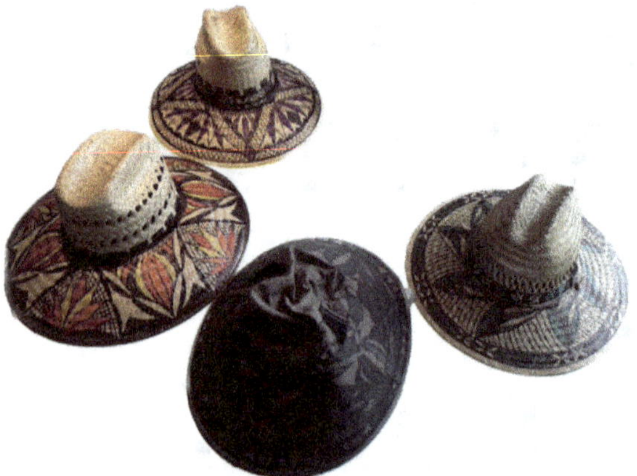

Figure 42: Among his artistic offerings, Nicholas King creates hats decorated with siapo motifs. Photo by Nicholas King.

Finding Siapo in Unexpected Ways

"My first introduction to siapo was lunch," Nick says when asked about his earliest memories of siapo.

In 1979, when Nick was 13 years old, the Jean P. Haydon Museum in Fagatogo hosted the American Samoa Arts Council Summer Youth Program. The program taught more than 100 students each summer about siapo, woodcarving, basket weaving, and storytelling, inviting the island's youth to connect with the traditional arts of Samoa.

However, for Nick and his friends, art wasn't what drew them towards the museum. They were motivated by the chocolate milk, hotdogs, and potato chips being served for lunch. The group of boys took a break from skateboarding to sneak into the lunch line at the youth program, but they were caught and ended up joining the art classes instead. A staff member handed Nick a piece of paper and a pencil and instructed him to join the group of students sitting in front of Mary Pritchard.

Mary taught the students traditional siapo patterns, and then instructed them to create a design of their own. When they finished sketching their designs on paper, she gave them a small siapo board, or u'a, on which to transfer their designs with pencil. She then gave them lama, o'a, ago, and loa dyes to complete their siapo pieces, providing guidance along the way with the help of the other teachers. Eventually, Mary pulled aside a few of the students who showed promise, including Nick, to complete larger boards and further develop their skills in the following weeks.

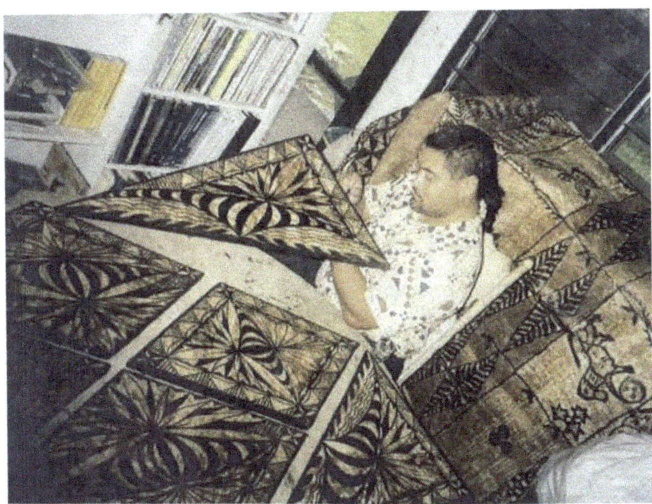

Figure 43: Nicholas King creating barkcloth art. Photo from the collection of Nicholas King.

Making Siapo, Making Mistakes

"I got into siapo by chance, but maybe I was always meant to be an artist," Nick says, thinking back on his early influences. He grew up with musicians, jewelry makers, and other creative family members, but the opportunity to learn from Mary Pritchard gave him the push he needed to explore his individual creativity and develop his skills as a visual artist.

Mary Pritchard taught Nick many lessons in his years as her student. One lesson that has remained with the artist over the decades is this: when making siapo, you will make mistakes.

"She told me that every siapo will have many mistakes," Nick remembers. "Your job is not to never make a mistake. Your job is to learn to work around your mistake, to accept it, and make it work in your art."

Participating in the arts programs on the island allowed Nick to keep learning about siapo and explore new places through the American Samoa Arts Council Choir. Nick was a part of the choir for five years and performed around the Pacific and the West Coast of the United States. Their performance involved young people acting out different parts of Samoan village life while the choir sang, and Nick was tasked with making siapo at the front of the stage during the show.

One year, the group traveled to Hawaii to perform, and while the other students in the choir were allowed free time, the siapo group was told to stay behind to work after a rehearsal.

"I sat there and pouted. All of my friends and my brothers were out at the mall," Nick says. His teenage-attitude caught the attention of Mary Pritchard, and she told him he could go to the mall if he didn't want to be there. He left to enjoy the mall, but later that evening he was pulled aside by Choir Director Pulefaasisina Palauni Tuiasosopo and Mary to talk.

"You're here for siapo. You can't dance, you can't sing, but you can do siapo," Palauni said. "If you don't want to do siapo, here's a ticket, you can go home tomorrow." Palauni pulled a ticket out of his pocket and held it out to Nick.

Mary Pritchard, who had been silent as Palauni spoke, looked at Nick and said, "You have talent. You can go somewhere with this, now go do the work." Her words left an indelible mark on the young artist.

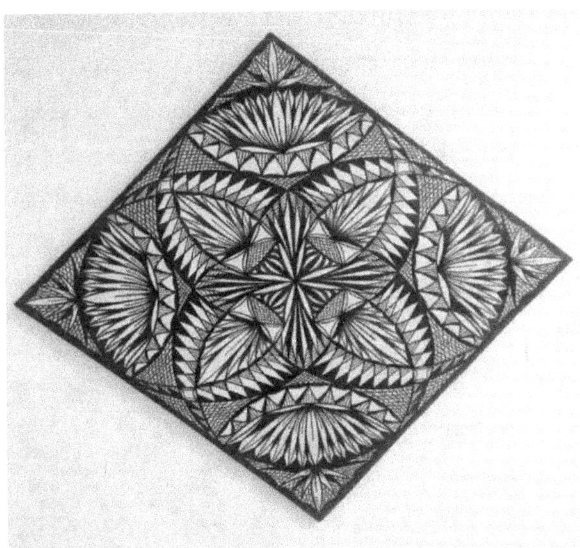

Figure 44: Siapo mamanu by Nick King using just the lama black dye. Photo by Nicholas King.

Putting in the Work

After his conversation with Mary and Palauni at 14, Nick's attitude changed. He embraced his artistic gifts and began to create as much as possible.

"From that day forward, I realized I have a gift and I need to put in the work and share it," Nick says. Sharing his siapo has taken many forms over the years, and it hasn't always involved the traditional materials of u'a and natural dyes. He has painted and drawn mamanu on countless household objects, and when working with a new material, Nick spends time researching best practices, deciding how to create an object that maintains the mamanu long-term.

While much of his art involves alternative materials, Nick returns to traditional siapo periodically to engage with the art form his ancestors developed. He receives barkcloth and dyes from Reggie Meredith Fitiao or buys from vendors at markets in Apia whenever he is inspired to work with natural materials or is commissioned by a buyer.

Nick has spent the last twenty years working as an oil company manager, but at the end of the day, he focuses his energy on his art. Working in the late evening and early morning allows Nick to lose himself in his work and use his art as a form of stress relief and emotional release.

Eventually, the artist wants to venture into three-dimensional designs with siapo patterns. For Nick, working with siapo and siapo patterns is a practice in innovation: "Our only limit is our imagination."

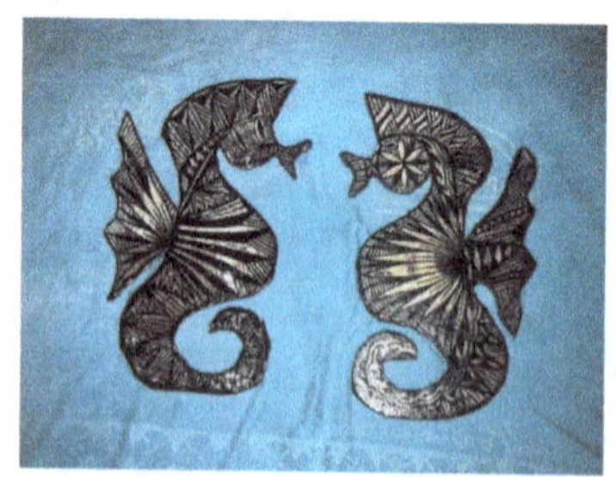

Figure 45: Two playful seahorse in siapo mamanu fashion by Nick King. Photo by Nicholas King.

Guidance for Aspiring Artists

For young people who are interested in becoming artists, Nick's advice focuses on mindset and mistakes. "Don't be afraid to make mistakes," he says. "Mistakes are the things that make you grow, make you develop, and make you stronger." Nick believes that in order to create art, you have to shift your mindset around mistakes and overcome your fears to share your creativity with the world.

"My hope is that siapo goes on forever and that every single generation has some tie back to our ancestors and the way we used to live," he says. "Siapo designs reflect the things we need to survive. It's nature. It's who we are."

In order for siapo to be carried forward by future generations, young people have to be willing to learn about the art form and develop deep connections with the role that siapo plays in Samoan culture.

Nick puts it plainly: "Be proud of where you come from, be proud of your culture, and have some hand in keeping your culture going."

Key Terms:

- **Commission**: A formal request to produce something (especially an artistic work) in exchange for payment from a specific client.

- **Innovation**: A new idea, method, or device. The introduction of something new.

Discussion Questions:

- Nick uses siapo motifs to create a wide range of art. His creativity and innovation has led to surprising and memorable experiences. What do you think are the benefits of creativity?

- Nick and his teachers all shared a simple truth: talent isn't enough, you have to put in the time and effort to create art. Do you agree with their opinion?

Chapter Twelve

STUDYING SIAPO IN MUSEUMS

M useums around the world display important objects in public exhibitions for visitors to learn from and explore. However, there is much more to a museum's collections. In fact, for many larger museums, less than ten percent of the collections' artifacts are on display (Bradley).

The items that are not on display are kept safe in storage. These storage facilities provide space for art conservators, anthropologists, researchers, cultural practitioners, and visitors to work with the precious objects behind the scenes.

There are museums around the world that house artifacts and artwork from American Samoa and Samoa. In the United States, the Smithsonian Institution, the Field Museum, and the museums at Harvard University and Yale University are among the list of museums that house siapo from the Samoan islands.

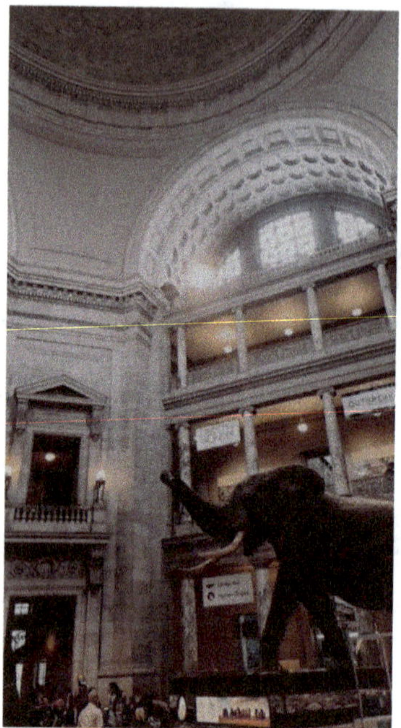

Figure 46: Entry hall of the Smithsonian Institution National Museum of Natural History. Photo by Mary Anne Peck.

How Museums Care for Siapo

Siapo has been cared for by the Samoan people for thousands of years, and over time these methods of care have developed and improved. Throughout the Pacific, tapa is normally folded or laid flat under mats or mattresses for storage. To care for tapa and preserve it for future use as clothing, gifts, or decoration, the barkcloth may be set out in the sun occasionally to keep the tapa fresh. In the past century, siapo makers in American Samoa have begun to coat their siapo with a polymer exterior varnish that protects the barkcloth from the elements and small insects.

In museums, there are several different methods for safely storing and caring for tapa to limit future damage and preserve the artwork for long periods of time.

According to the University of Glasgow, an institution that is home to a large collection of tapa, storing barkcloth by laying it flat is a preferred method ("Care Guidelines, Tapa"). This is because folding a tapa that is in long-term storage can cause damage where the creasing becomes fragile with time. Museums use acid-free paper and white cotton cloth to layer tapa that are laid flat in boxes or drawers. This storage method allows for researchers to safely move the siapo, especially if a tapa is heavily damaged.

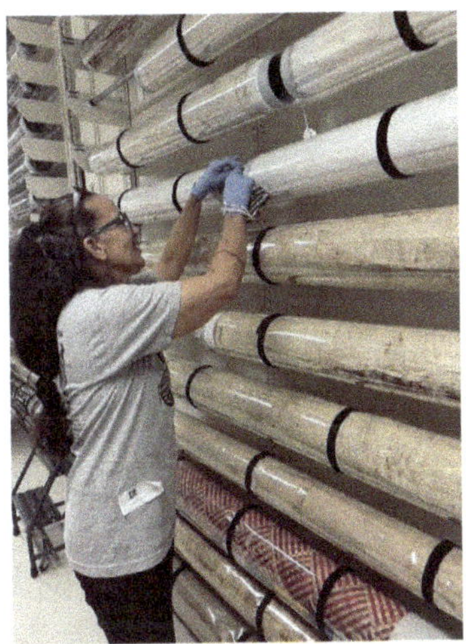

Figure 47: Reggie Meredith finds her rolled tapa, Cat. No. 358466 (siapo mamanu) at the Field Museum of Chicago. Photo by Mary Anne Peck.

Another method of storing siapo is by rolling. Larger tapa are difficult to store flat, so to avoid folding, many museums will roll large tapa on tubes with acid-free paper. Once rolled, the tapa is covered with a clear, plastic sheet to provide extra protection. This method allows for the safe storage of large tapa and minimizes damage caused by creasing and folding.

On top of using the best storage practices, museums also monitor the temperature and humidity levels in exhibits and in storage rooms. They may also limit direct exposure to light, keeping artwork like siapo in dark places, such as shelves or covered halls, to limit any breakdown of the barkcloth or dyes.

Studying Siapo Mamanu

Siapo mamanu, the freehand style of siapo, can be found across the United States. The dyes used in siapo mamanu–lama, o'a, ago, and loa–can change drastically with time, and some museums are exploring new ways to study these siapo to learn more about the artists' original designs.

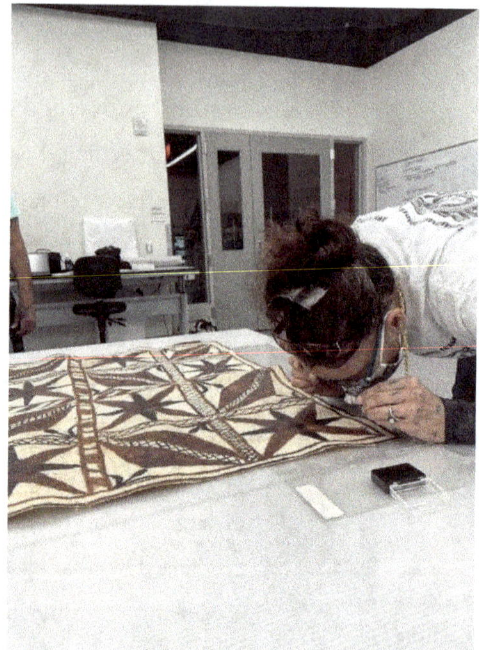

Figure 48: Reggie gets close to observe the fibers and dyes of older siapo. Photo by Mary Anne Peck.

The Yale Peabody Museum at Yale University is studying siapo using photography. Photographing the items in a museum's collection is a standard practice, but Yale is taking this documentation one step further: they are capturing infrared and ultraviolet images of the barkcloth ("Tapa Cloths from the Peabody Museum").

In 2015, Catherine Sease, a senior conservator at the Yale Peabody Museum, worked with assistants, interns, and volunteers to assess, repair, photograph, and rehouse over 200 Pacific tapa in the museum's collection. Part of this process involved working with a professional photographer, William A. Guth, to capture high-resolution, ultraviolet (UV), and infrared images of each tapa. These images showed layers to the tapa that weren't visible to the human eye.

For example, the siapo shown below is a siapo mamanu from Samoa. The maker of this siapo mamanu used the lama and o'a to create her design. While the black dye, lama, remains the same over the years, the brown dye, o'a, changes with time. As the o'a on this siapo darkened, the designs in the center of the siapo were covered, and it became hard to distinguish the lama from the o'a.

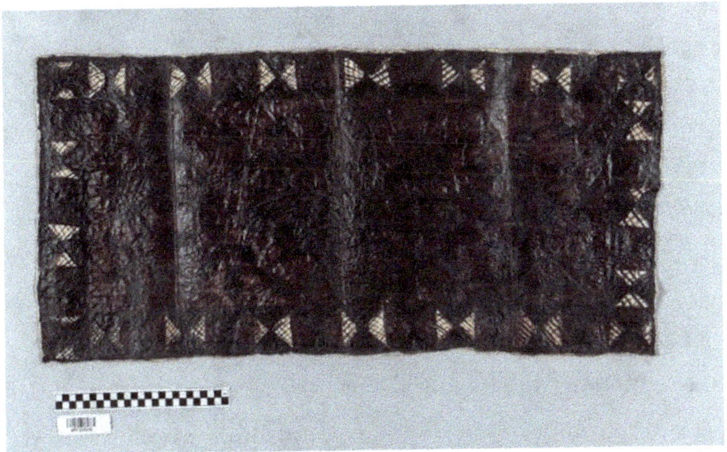

Figure 49: A siapo mamanu that has darkened with age, making the pattern unidentifiable. Yale Peabody Museum, Cat. No. 20330. Guth, W., 2015.

However, when this same siapo mamanu is photographed in a way that shows more than the visible light, using UV and infrared photography, researchers are able to see more of the original design and drawings that lay underneath the darkened and aged dyes.

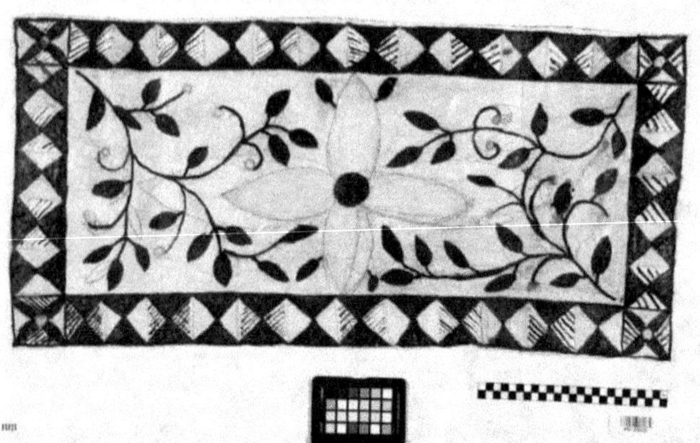

Figure 50: Advanced photography techniques help museum professionals at Yale University uncover the patterns on aged tapa. Yale Peabody Museum, Cat. No. 020330. Guth, W., 2015.

These innovations allow museum professionals and cultural practitioners to learn more about the ways that Samoan siapo has been made throughout history and how the art form has changed over time.

Studying Siapo Tasiga

As discussed in previous chapters, siapo tasiga, also known as siapo elei, is barkcloth art made by rubbing designs onto processed paper mulberry bark. A design is carved into a wooden board called an upeti, and then elei, red river rocks, are ground into a fine powder and rubbed into the fabric to reveal the pattern.

While river rocks are the traditional material used by siapo makers, there have been changes and trends throughout history as siapo makers explored other materials. For example, siapo makers in the early 1900s experimented with food coloring, mercurochrome, and a blue laundry liquid, brought by U.S. sailors to whiten their uniforms, as a new ink for their artwork. Museums study the different materials used to create siapo tasiga, including the dyes on the barkcloth and the carved boards.

During a visit to the Field Museum, I was able to witness an important moment in the study of a siapo tasiga in their collection. Su'a Uilisone and Reggie Fitiao were studying a bright blue siapo tasiga when the collections manager, Christopher Phillip, suddenly left the room. When he returned, he was holding a carved upeti. The pattern on the upeti was an exact match to the siapo on the examining table.

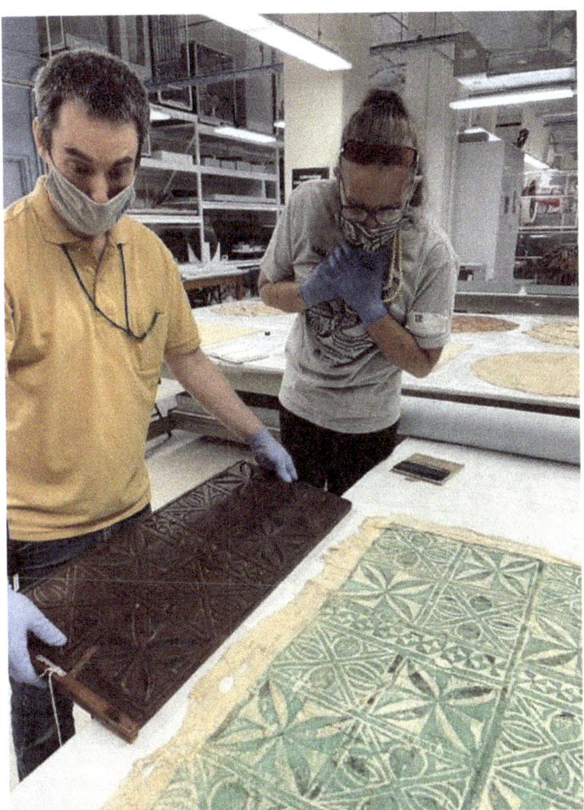

Figure 51: An amazing moment in the Field Museum conservation lab with Collection manager Chris Philipp. Photo by Mary Anne Peck.

These items, the siapo (Cat. No. 167181) and the upeti (Cat. No. 361558), were collected in two different decades by two different people before being given to the museum. Upon further research, our team was able to find pictures in the museum's archives that show Samoan women using the upeti to make siapo.

At the end of 2023, Christopher Phillip visited American Samoa to talk with siapo makers about a future exhibit in Chicago. While here, the team from the Field Museum conducted research in local archives and spoke with students at American Samoa Community College about the ongoing relationship between the museum and American Samoa.

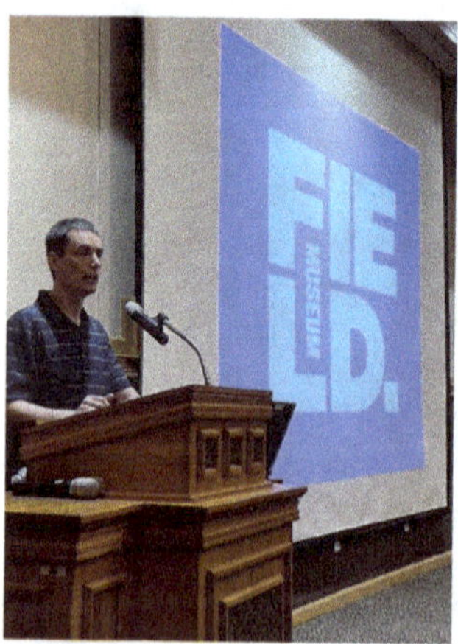

Figure 52: Christopher Philipp speaks at American Samoa Community College during his 2023 visit. Photo by Fynn Peck.

Who Can Study the Siapo Stored in Museum Collections?

Museum staff are not the only people who can study the siapo in collections. Museums often invite cultural practitioners, writers, and researchers to study the siapo and other measina in their collections.

Providing access to the collections is a part of a wider trend of co-curation—a process in which museums and the communities that their collections originate from work together to study artifacts and share important stories with the world.

When we began planning the research trip that inspired this book, our team reached out to curators and conservators at museums around the United States and were welcomed with open arms.

These museums also showcase their collections through digital archives on the internet. While researchers can make appointments to study artwork in person at museums, you can also explore their digital collections from the comfort of your own home and read notes left by conservators, collections managers, and other museum professionals.

Providing access, both physically and digitally, is one way museums like the Yale Peabody Museum and the Field Museum are working to create safe spaces for the measina of Samoa.

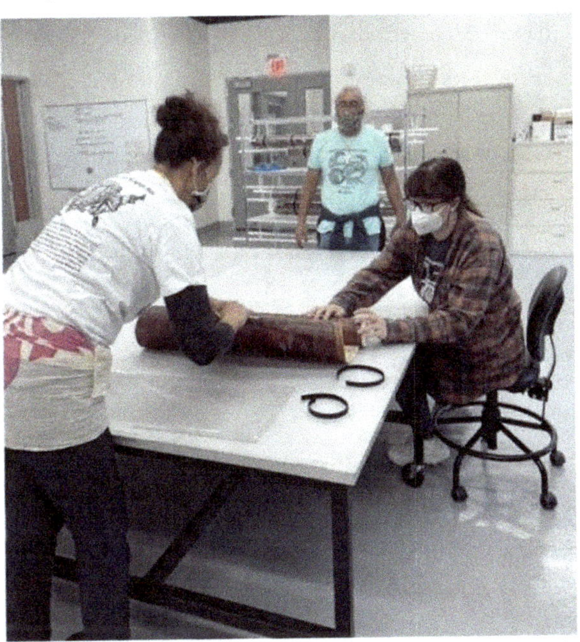

Figure 53: Mary Anne Peck, Su'a Uilisone Fitiao, and Reggie Meredith Fitiao carefully roll a siapo at the Yale Peabody Museum. Photo by Rebekah DeAngelo.

Key Terms:

- **Polymer exterior varnish**: A waterproof, UV-resistant, clear coating that can be used as a sealant.

- **Infrared**: When used in reference to imaging, infrared describes images that capture light outside the visible spectrum at its red end.

- **Ultraviolet**: When used in reference to imaging, ultraviolet describes images that capture light outside the visible spectrum at its violet end.

- **Co-curation**: A practice in modern museums that involves the inclusion of source communities and outside experts in the curatorial process and creation of exhibits.

Discussion Questions:

- There are many ways siapo is studied in museums. What method of study interested you most in this chapter? Photography, digital archives, hands-on study?

Chapter Thirteen

Co-Curation with Cultural Practitioners

Christopher Philipp, Collections Manager

Christopher Philipp is a collections manager at the Field Museum in Chicago, Illinois. The Field Museum, founded in 1893 and originating from the World's Columbian Exposition, is home to nearly 40 million cultural artifacts and natural history specimens representing the disciplines of anthropology, botany, geology, and zoology. These collections are cared for by a variety of museum professionals, including curators, conservators, lab technicians, and more.

At The Field Museum, Chris works as a collections manager in the museum's Gantz Family Collections Center and directly assists with the care of the Anthropology collections from the Pacific islands.

Chris' work often brings him into contact with the measina of Samoa and modern cultural practitioners from Oceania.

Getting His Foot in the Door

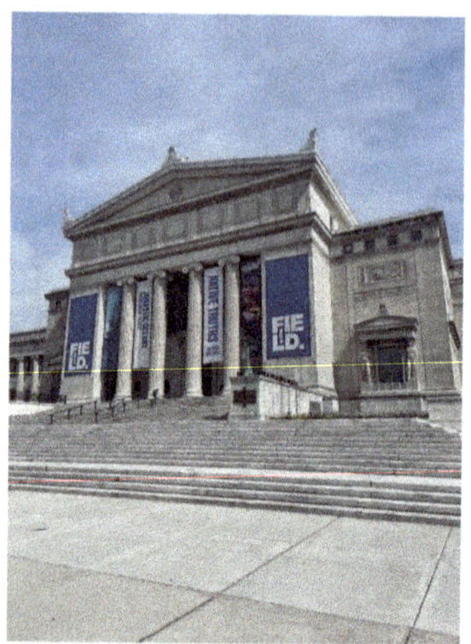

Figure 54: The Field Museum of Chicago is home to a collection of barkcloth from across the Pacific. Photo by Mary Anne Peck.

"My dad was an antique dealer and my aunt was an artist," Chris says, thinking back on the influences that brought him to museum work. "I've always been interested in the stories that old things can tell."

An interest in history and geography impacted Chris's undergraduate degree, leading him to pursue a major in anthropology and minors in museum studies and ethnomusicology at Beloit College, two hours north of Chicago in the state of Wisconsin.

While earning his degree, Chris worked at his college's library. Upon graduation, he returned to Chicago and began working at the Ryerson Library at the Art Institute. Interested in learning about musical instruments residing at the Field Museum, Chris decided to call the museum to ask about available volunteer positions.

"I called the Field Museum to see if there were any opportunities to work with musical instruments in the collections," he remembers. "The Volunteer Coordinator connected me on the phone with the curator of the African collections, and after five minutes of talking, he invited me to become a new volunteer. That's how I got my foot in the door." Chris says, "the best way to find out if you like working in museums is by trying things out as an intern or volunteer."

Soon, a job opened up to work with a team to remove all of the Central and South American items from an old exhibit dating from the 1950s.

"Taking the objects off from the display, making storage mounts for them, organizing them–that was my job for the next two years," Chris remembers. "Before that project was over, the Field Museum promoted me to a permanent position as Collections Manager in 2000."

In 2005, the museum moved him to a new role as the Regenstein collections manager. "I took on the duties of helping to care for cultural heritage items from the Pacific Islands, and that's part of what I still do today."

Working as a Collections Manager

Collections managers are responsible for many different aspects of the care and management of a museum's collections and storage spaces. These museum professionals manage collections in storage and on display and facilitate access to the collections for a variety of visitors. They also take steps to document the collections and to care for and preserve items.

"My favorite part of being a collections manager is the multiple hats you wear and the many different people that you encounter along the way," Chris says. "Your primary duty is to help the museum care for the collections and provide access to the collections."

Caring for a museum collection, especially one at a museum of this size, is a monumental task. Chris and his colleagues keep the collection's inventory up to date and conduct condition checks as a part of The Field Museum's preventative conservation measures.

"Where a conservator will do more intensive and specialized treatments to reverse or stabilize the condition of an item, collections managers are mostly trying to ensure that items are stored and handled properly and reside in a stable environment," Chris explains. Chris and his colleagues work to create a safe environment for the items in their care, including building proper housing for objects to minimize handling and maintaining the best temperature and humidity for different materials.

As a part of this work, Chris has set and maintained an impressive goal for himself–since 2016, he has built an average of over 2,000 storage boxes and mounts for collections items per year.

Beyond caring for the collection, Chris is also responsible for providing access to the collection. This access often involves working closely with cultural practitioners.

"We are trying to increase access to collections, but doing that mindfully, respectfully and in consultation with the communities who are the original makers and owners of those items that are now cared for by the Field Museum," Chris says.

Caring for the Measina of Samoa

Part of Chris' job is caring for the measina, precious things, of Samoa, and in the 25 years he has worked at the Field Museum, the institution has undergone massive changes with the goal of providing better care for the collections.

Twenty-three years ago, the museum began construction of the Collections Resource Center (CRC). This facility added 180,000 square feet to the museum, creating a temperature-controlled space for large portions of the Field Museum's collections to be stored safely and accessed easier.

In this new space, Chris and his colleagues have worked to care for Samoan material culture since their relocation there about fifteen years ago.

The museum currently cares for about 1,000 pieces of tapa, and many of those tapa are Samoan siapo. For three years, several Field Museum Regenstein internships were dedicated to working with J. P. Brown, a conservator, and Chris to photograph each tapa and roll them onto archival materials for safe storage and better accessibility.

Once the siapo was documented and rolled, they began to work on the woven mats in the collection. While the COVID-19 pandemic interrupted their work, the team was able to document and safely store about 1,000 mats from Oceania over the course of another three years.

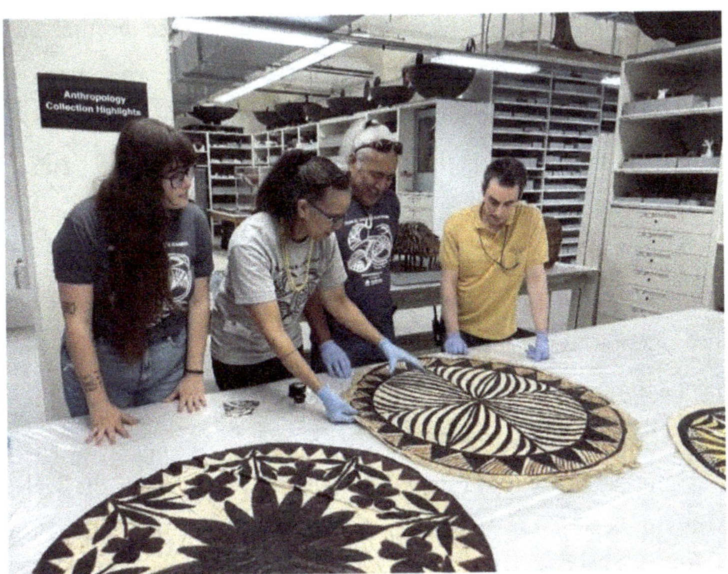

Figure 55: Mary, Reggie, Uilisone, and Chris study a circular siapo (Cat. Nos. 167186 and 167187) at The Field Museum in 2022. Photo by Julia Kennedy.

The CRC is where the Pacific collections of tapa and woven mats are housed, but it is also a space for cultural practitioners and researchers to interact with the items in the collection. For example, in 2022, siapo makers from American Samoa were able to visit the museum and study the siapo in Chicago.

While this visit occurred in 2022, the relationship between Chris and the artists of American Samoa began in 2011.

Traveling to American Samoa

In 2011, Dr. John Terrell, the curator of the Field Museum's Pacific collection, sent Chris to American Samoa. This trip took Chris beyond the duties he performs day-to-day as a collections manager. It was time for him to put on a different hat and perform curatorial duties.

Chris' goal in American Samoa was to meet and talk with people about the collection and extend invitations to share together and hopefully create opportunities for collaboration. The trip started off slow, but he met a professor at American Samoa Community College who gave him a bit of helpful advice. He was told he needed to meet Reggie Meredith.

"She picked me up off the side of the road, and the first thing I saw was her dog, Emo, sitting in her lap," Chris says, remembering his introduction to the siapo maker. "I told her we had 600 items from Samoa in our collection [at the time] that we were trying to care for and we wanted to see what we can do together."

He told Reggie that there were close to 100 siapo in the Field Museum's collection, and as they drove down the curved roads along the coast of American Samoa, she asked, "Do you have any siapo mamanu?"

The museum only had a few of the freehand siapo, and when she asked why they didn't have more than that, Chris had a very simple answer: "Because you haven't made it for us yet."

"That's when it dawned on Reggie that I wasn't representing the typical museum of the past, going out and trying to buy everyone's old things to bring back to the museum," Chris remembers. "I was there to share, to listen, and to hopefully 'collect' a new friendship that could develop into a partnership. And that's what we've built on ever since."

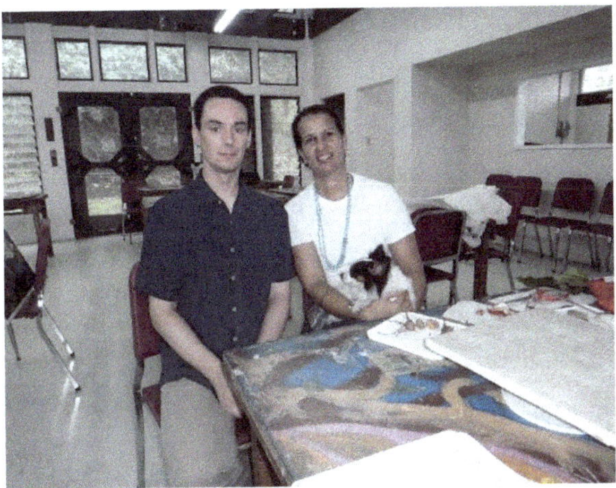

Figure 56: Chris, Reggie, and Emo pose for a photo during Chris' initial visit to American Samoa in 2011. Photo from the collection of Christopher Philipp.

Chris, in consultation with Reggie, commissioned siapo pieces on the spot. Reggie, Su'a Uilisone, Maria Walker, Patrick Mafo'e, and Dylan Bruce created eight pieces that were added to The Field Museum's collection with the goal of continuing the story of siapo, bringing it from the past and into the present.

How Can Museums Facilitate Storytelling?

Through Chris's travels and work, he has met modern-day artists and cultural practitioners who are working to save their traditions and share them with the next generation.

During his visit to Rarotonga in 2010, he met a family of barkcloth makers who spent their days trying to keep important cultural practices alive.

"On the island of Mangaia, the Papatua family organized a workshop for folks on the island to make barkcloth from the aerial roots of the banyan tree," Chris remembers. "I brought the piece of barkcloth that we prepared and beat together during the workshop back to the museum for the collection. It is one of many items that represent the story of people trying to keep their cultural art and knowledge alive."

The Papatua family in Rarotonga and the siapo makers of American Samoa share a struggle that communities around the world are experiencing—the fight to keep their important cultural practices alive.

Chris has witnessed this struggle first hand, and he believes that museums can step up to help.

"A museum can help in this process by connecting, by doing things differently, by acting as a facilitator that promotes sharing and learning between communities, the museum, and its visitors," Chris says. His words touch on a practice that is becoming more common in modern museums, a process called co-curation.

Co-curation is a process of partnership between a museum and the source communities where items in the museum's collection originated. For example, the Field Museum has long worked with the Maori community from Tokomaru Bay, Aotearoa in the restoration and rededication of Ruatepupuke II, a wharenui, or meeting house, originally built in 1881. The museum and the Maori community have collaborated to define the use and interpretation of this house and the museum's marae as they reside on display in the Field Museum's Regenstein Halls of the Pacific today.

Working with the community in ways like this helps the museum to prioritize culturally competent storytelling, and to uplift the communities with direct ties to the items on display.

Co-curation was not always a part of museum work. In fact, for much of museum history, curators have built collections by buying old objects from local people or stealing objects outright. Curators then returned to their museums and told the story of the "exotic" people they saw on their journeys. The goal of co-curation is to acknowledge these past practices and move towards a better path that involves sharing the stories that are important to communities around the world.

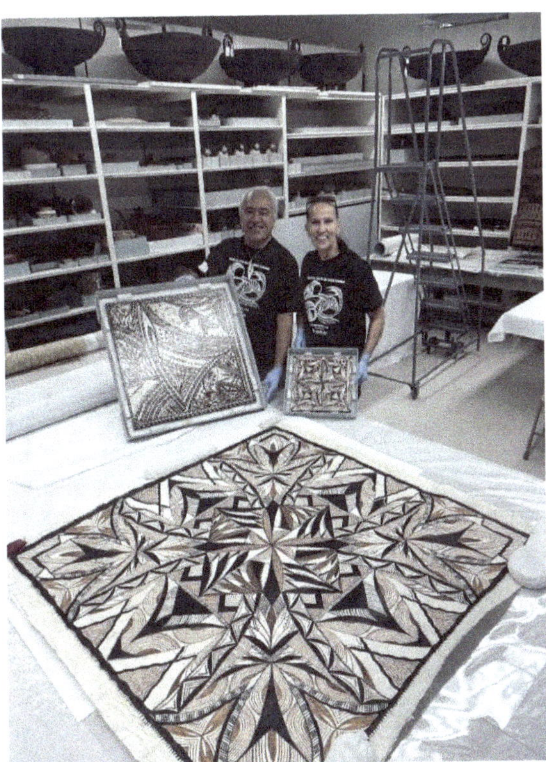

Figure 57: Su'a Uilisone and Reggie pose with their artwork that has been accessioned into the Oceanic collection of The Field Museum. Photo by Mary Anne Peck.

So, how can the Field Museum facilitate storytelling? A good start is by connecting with the people who are maintaining and teaching cultural practices in their communities.

"There's this theme, and it's not just Samoa, it's not just siapo," Chris says, reflecting on the cultural practices around the world that are threatened. "While some are disappearing, some are as strong as ever and some are adapting and changing, perhaps just as cultural practices also changed and evolved in the past."

Most importantly, these cultural practices are being carried forward by creators who are working to teach others in their communities and around the world about the traditional artforms of their people.

"We want to help cultural practitioners to tell their stories and keep the momentum going, both on their front and ours," Chris says. "We are working every day to build a better museum, a more inclusive museum, a museum that is a facilitator for these conversations. By changing the way we think about how museums share and work with communities and people across the world, not as projects, but as part of a process with equal stakes in the management of the global heritage museums are privileged to help care for, we thereby change the definition of what it is to be a museum."

Key Terms:

- **Collections manager**: A museum professional who manages the items in the collection through preventative conservation and community access.

- **Museum studies**: The science or profession of museum organization and management.

- **Ethnomusicology**: The study of music from around the world, including the study of musical instruments.

- **Curator**: A person who oversees or manages a place (such as a museum) that offers exhibits.

- **Storage boxes/mounts**: Items built to better store and display museum collections.

- **Preventative conservation**: The act of preventing further deterioration by controlling the storage environment of museum objects.

- **Archival materials**: Materials such as acid-free paper and storage containers that help conservators to safely store fragile materials.

Discussion Questions:

- Co-curation involves collaboration between museums and source communities. How do these two groups work together to care for collections?

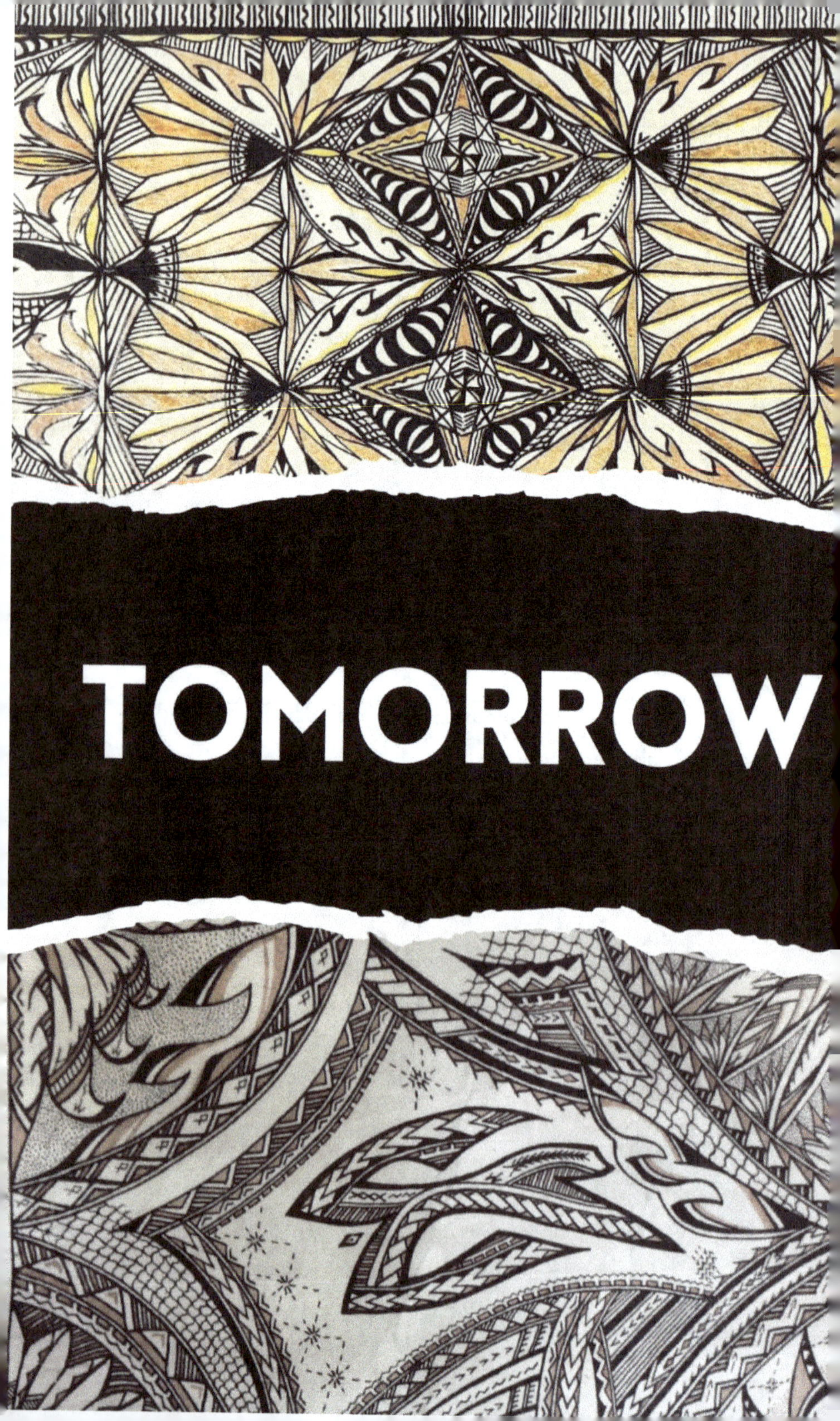
TOMORROW

Making Art That Moves The Audience

Talanoa Lagafuaina, Artist and Siapo Student

When talking about the future of visual art and siapo in American Samoa, it's important to look to the young artists of our island. One such artist is Talanoa Lagafuaina, a 16 year old from Nu'uuli Village who has made waves across the island with his paintings.

Talanoa's art is surrealist, drawing inspiration from reality and interpreting it without directly copying it. His artistic process is inspired by the idea of ka'a (an escape from reality). Ka'a moves him to think of his life and his art in new ways.

Learning from Siapo Makers

In 2021, Talanoa had the opportunity to participate in the Fa'asamoa Arts' Children's Siapo Workshop, where he spent a month learning about siapo from Su'a Uilisone Fitiao and Reggie Meredith Fitiao. Learning about siapo in that environment had a strong impact on his paintings.

"Siapo has helped me to connect more with my culture, and not in a way that feels forced. After learning about siapo, you learn that the people who created siapo in the past didn't do it just because it was a tradition," Talanoa says. "Siapo was their own way of expressing themselves and seeing the world around them through siapo."

Initially, Talanoa didn't feel inspired to include what he learned about siapo into his paintings, and avoided including siapo motifs. However, after his understanding of siapo began to deepen, his opinion shifted.

"After learning about siapo from a siapo maker, you learn that these symbols are not just for decoration. They mean something in their own right." Talanoa says, reflecting on his relationship with siapo. "They have their own meanings, and I can place them in a painting knowing what they mean and what they express and how they add to the feeling of the piece."

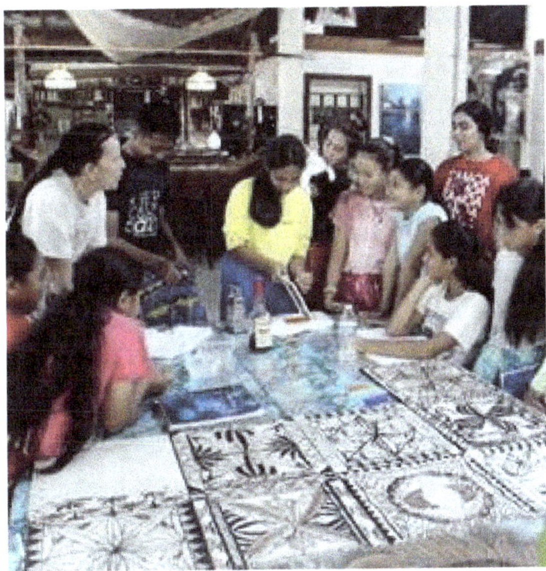

Figure 58: Students, including Talanoa, study siapo in Leone through workshops provided by Fa'asamoa Arts. Photo by Fynn Peck.

Drawing Inspiration from Samoan Culture

For Talanoa, his culture greatly inspires his art. He draws inspiration from the fa'alavelave of Samoa and the memories he associates with these events. One instance he acknowledges is the way the emotional climate of funerals in Samoa differ from the American idea of grief.

"Here, when a family member passes away, it's different. The family is grieving, we know they are grieving, but they need to be very stoic in those difficult times," Talanoa says. The subtlety of grief in Samoa continues to draw the artist's attention, and he tries to portray that subtlety in his paintings.

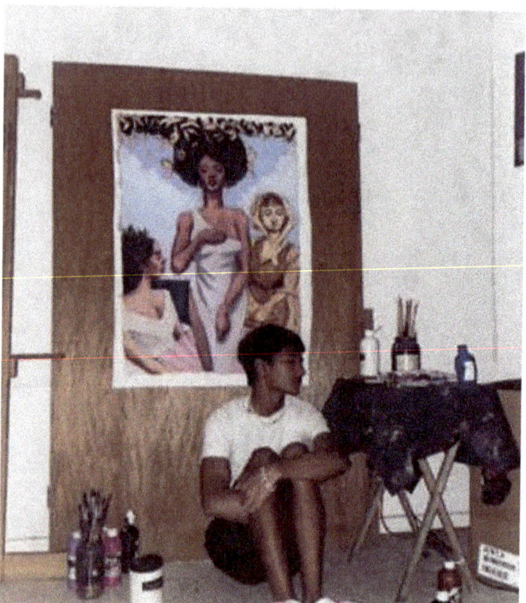

Figure 59: Talanoa posing with one of his paintings.
Photo from the collection of Talanoa Lagafuaina.

In Talanoa's short career, he has overcome many challenges, with the biggest one being the weight of public approval. Many art buyers and clients in the region expect beautiful depictions of the mountains, beaches, and people of American Samoa in Talanoa's work, but those paintings aren't in line with what the young artist is working towards.

"A lot of people want to paint the beautiful Samoan landscape, but I want to try to do something different. I want to subvert the expectation that people have in their head of what a beautiful painting is," Talanoa says. "I want there to be more substance than beauty in my art."

Just as the siapo motifs are more than simple designs, Talanoa wants his art to be about more than what the audience sees on the surface.

"I want to make art that moves you."

As a 16 year old, Talanoa is starting to make plans for his future, including exploring options for earning an art degree from a school like the Rhode Island School of Design.

"In terms of my art, I'm going to go where the wind takes me," Talanoa says when asked about his artistic plans. "I started off doing what everyone expected of me, but now I've changed my direction, and I like where I'm going right now. My artwork is being tailored to my liking, rather than the public opinion."

The Future of Visual Art in American Samoa

Talanoa believes that the approach to the visual arts is different in American Samoa when compared to Samoa. The artist believes this difference is due to the Americanized culture of American Samoa.

"In Western Samoa, their art—all forms—is alive and breathing and thriving. But American Samoa is overly Americanized, and there is a lower level of priority on the arts of our island."

One way to remedy this situation, according to the young artist, is for the leadership of the island to prioritize visual arts.

"There is a lot of overlooked potential on our island for the visual arts," Talanoa says. "There aren't enough paths for people on our island to pursue art. The artists of our island have to find their own way—I found my own way, but I want others to be able to uncover their potential with visual art."

Talanoa believes that the first step for improving the state of the visual arts in American Samoa, specifically siapo, is for community leaders and organizations to raise awareness and focus on youth-centered siapo programs.

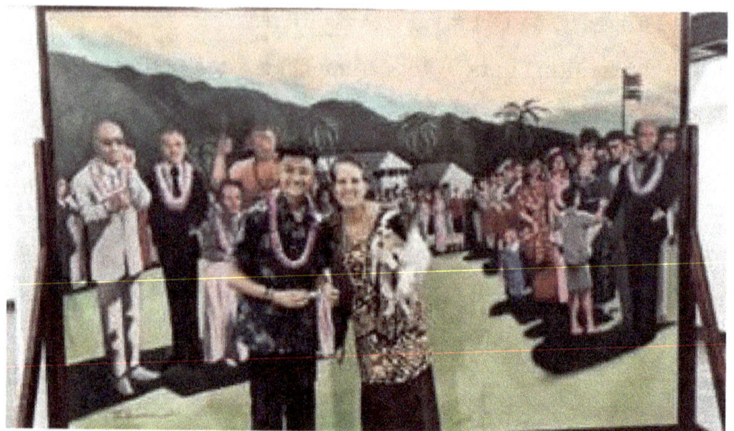

Figure 60: Talanoa and Reggie Meredith Fitiao pose with Talanoa's painting at Jean P. Haydon Museum. Photo from the collection of Talanoa Lagafuaina.

"Basketball and football haven't always been here. They were brought here and gained popularity. But siapo? It's always been here, and it may fade from our island if we don't do something," Talanoa says. "The leadership of our island obviously cares about protecting our culture, with the work they are doing to preserve our language, so they must also care about this visual part of our culture."

When asked, Talanoa was happy to provide advice for other young people interested in learning about siapo and creating art. His advice can be summed up in one sentence: be willing to learn.

"Don't feel uncomfortable about not knowing everything about our own siapo, our artform. As long as you are willing to learn, you will be taken in with open arms and you will learn something," Talanoa says. "You may not go on to create siapo for the rest of your life, but as long as that knowledge is in your head, that is one more person who knows about their own culture—about siapo."

Key Terms:

·   **Surrealism**: A movement in the arts that focuses on positive expression and the defiance of reality and reason. It came about initially as a reaction to the horrors of World Wars I and II (1914-1945). Artists associated with this period include Salvador Dali and Frida Kahlo.

·   **Ka'a**: A Samoan term for time spent physically escaping from daily responsibilities or mentally escaping from reality.

·   **Fa'alavelave**: Situations that require the attention of the family (such as a funeral).

Discussion Questions:

·   Talanoa finds inspiration in the fa'alavelave (specifically the funeral traditions) of Samoa. In what other ways can we find inspiration in grief, sadness, etc.?

·   What role should young people play in the future of siapo?

CHAPTER FIFTEEN

STRENGTHENING CULTURAL CONNECTION THROUGH ART

PUA TOFAEONO, ARTIST, ENTREPRENEUR, SIAPO MAKER

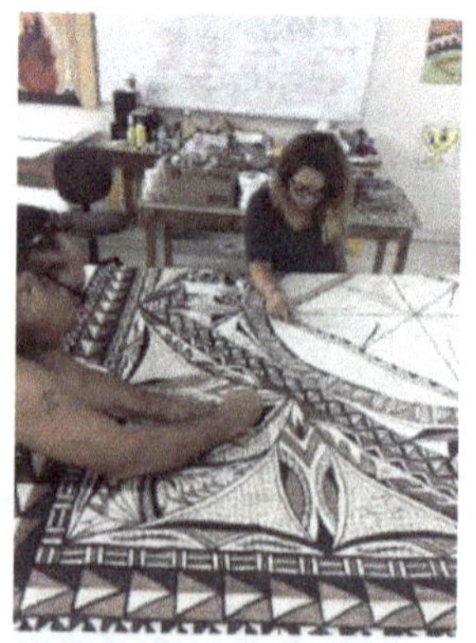

Figure 61: Pua Tofaeono and Su'a Uilisone Fitiao work on a siapo mamanu.

Pua Tofaeono has built her business as an artist, designer, and photographer since she was 21 years old. Her murals can be found around American Samoa and her paintings hang on the walls of local businesses and homes.

An Artist's Beginnings

Now 27 years old, Pua has grown to be a prolific artist and creative. Looking back,

Pua remembers when her dream of being an artist first began—her fourth grade art class.

"I've been interested in art from a young age, but I didn't know I wanted to be an artist until I was nine years old. I dressed as my art teacher for Halloween, and I knew I wanted to be her when I grew up," Pua says.

In her teens, a couple of months before her high school graduation, Pua's family moved from Maryland to American Samoa. She didn't grow up in American Samoa and didn't speak the language, so the move left her feeling uncertain.

"I told my dad I wanted to go home," she remembers. "He told me I was already home. I didn't realize then how right he was."

Pua grew up in a predominantly white area of Maryland. She grew up in a part of the world that didn't have much representation or understanding of her Polynesian roots, leaving her feeling detached from her own culture.

"I didn't realize how disconnected I was from myself as a Samoan. I had a bit of an identity crisis when I got here," Pua says, thinking back on her first few months in American Samoa.

Her childhood was far removed from Samoa and the Samoan language, but Pua soon found a place where she began to piece together parts of her identity as a Samoan: Professor Reggie Meredith Fitiao's Indigenous Art Forms class at the American Samoa Community College.

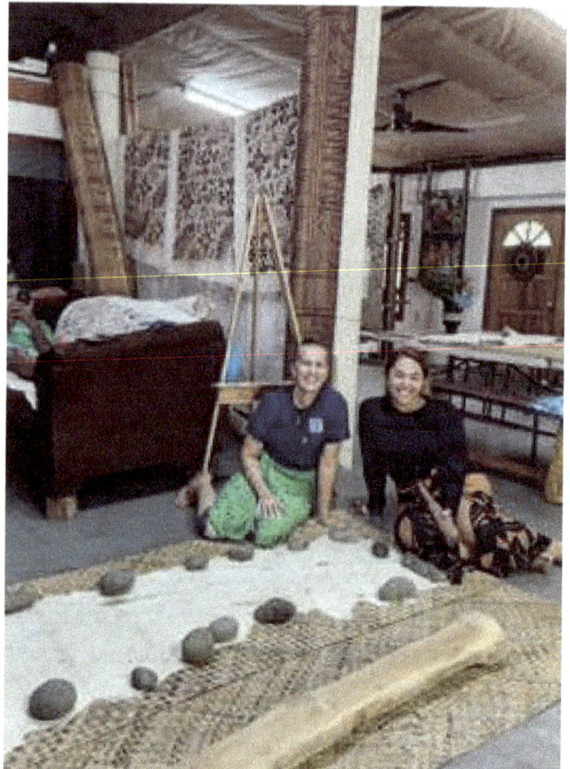

Figure 62: Reggie and Pua pose in Reggie's studio in Leone. Photo by Pua Tofaeono.

"That was my first time feeling so connected to our culture. I felt like I actually belonged," Pua says. "Reggie said that before there was written language, we used art to tell our stories. And as someone who didn't understand Samoan at the time, it helped me connect to our ancestors in a way I hadn't before."

For Pua, making art and learning about siapo became a way for her to connect with her heritage and make her voice heard.

In class, she was able to learn how the materials for siapo are harvested from nature and how they are prepared to create art. The time she spent scraping bark from trees and preparing siapo dyes helped her to connect with her ancestors and with the island itself.

Drawing Inspiration from Siapo

As she continues to grow as an artist, one of Pua's goals is to dedicate more of her time to learning from local siapo makers. In pursuit of this goal, Pua has begun to spend time each week with Reggie Meredith Fitiao, learning every step of the siapo making process from a master of the art form.

"I would like to see a revival in siapo making. Our art is sacred, and I want to be a part of that revival," Pua says. "We need people we can trust to carry siapo forward for future generations."

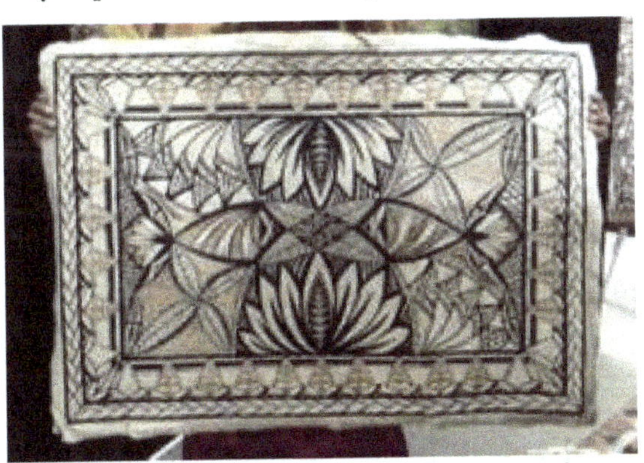

*Figure 63: A siapo mamanu created by Pua Tofaeono.
Photo by Pua Tofaeono.*

Pua has also found ways to include siapo in her other creative works, such as painting and design. Tatau motifs are a common occurrence in designs used by Samoan brands, but Pua prefers to use siapo motifs, bringing her indigenous arts education into her work. Siapo motifs can also be found in Pua's paintings and murals.

One siapo motif that Pua feels a deep connection with is the fa'aatualoa, the pattern that portrays the centipede.

"For many people, the fa'aatualoa means overcoming pain and hardships, and having strength through it all," Pua says, reflecting on the impact that specific siapo pattern has had on her and the story it tells. Understanding the siapo motifs is one way Pua uses her art as a pathway for storytelling and connecting with the artists who came before her.

You Don't Have to be a Starving Artist

Pua knows that becoming a self-employed artist is not the safest career choice a person can make. With this career, there are no stable paychecks, no supervisors to keep you on track–you are responsible for everything. In addition to the possible instability, there is also a lot of societal pressure that can quickly discourage a young artist from pursuing their calling.

"Don't be discouraged," Pua says when asked about her advice for young artists. "Being an artist is not a job most people want their child to pursue, but if this is what you want to do, move forward and work on your craft."

Pua is faced with uncertain reactions from others when talking about her art.

"When I tell people I'm an artist, some just think I'm unemployed. Typically it's the elders who worry about me. But you don't have to be a starving artist, you can thrive doing what you love." Pua encourages young artists to explore the ways they can support themselves as adults while creating art.

She also remembers the early days of her artistic career, being 21 years old and having no clue how to run her business. But she challenged herself to learn new skills and over time her business has evolved into something meaningful.

"If you are naturally gifted, don't just stop there. Keep challenging yourself," Pua advises young artists. "If this is your passion and what you want to pursue in life, it doesn't have to be a side hustle–go full force. The life of an artist can be unpredictable but it's such a beautiful journey."

Bringing Samoan Culture to the World

For Pua, one of the most amazing parts of being an artist is the impact her work can have on people she has never met.

"Making art isn't just about making money," Pua says. "It's about connecting with people in new ways."

These connections tend to sneak up on the artist. She may meet a person in the United States who has admired her art from afar via social media, or see someone in Fiji or New Zealand wearing clothing that features her designs.

"Through art, you can carry our culture beyond our shores," Pua believes. Art, dance, music, and fashion–Pua believes these are ways that Samoan people can share Samoan culture to places her ancestors never dreamed of.

Pua believes that while Samoa is a small group of islands on the map, the cultural impact of these islands is far-reaching. There are artists, actors, musicians, and athletes who uphold Samoan culture in a respectful way, showing it to the world.

"When our ancestors were navigating the oceans, I don't know if they ever knew just how far we would go in this world," Pua reflects on the perseverance her ancestors had as they traveled the largest ocean in the world. "Their perseverance then, and our perseverance now, is inspiring."

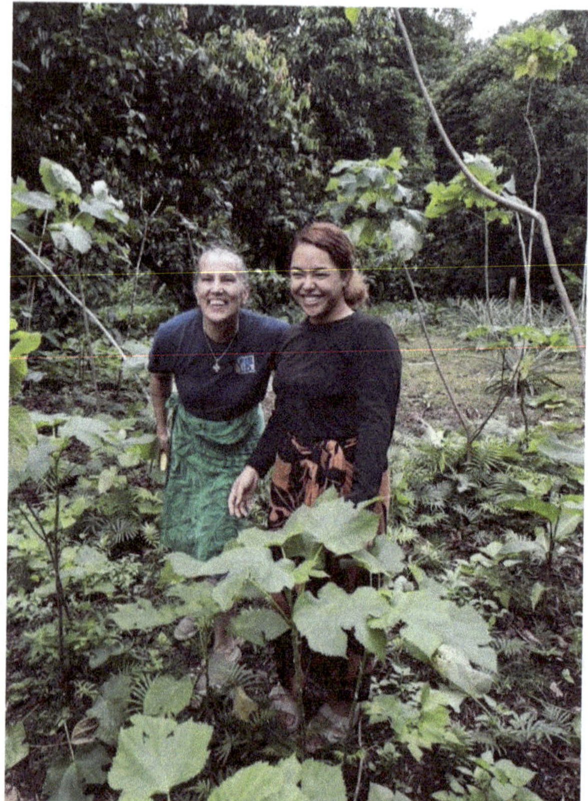

Figure 64: Reggie and Pua spend time together collecting siapo materials. Photo by Su'a Uilisone Fitiao.

This connection between the Samoans of the past and the present is part of what draws Pua to art forms like siapo.

"Art that is made from such a natural form is alive. You can feel the energy from it, you can feel the spirit," Pua believes in the mana, the spiritual power that siapo can carry. "Can you imagine the hands who made this? The artists who aren't here anymore?"

For Pua, carrying on the lineage of the Samoan artists of yesterday motivates her as she creates art and participates in siapo projects.

"American Samoa has my heart and soul. No matter where I go, I'll call American Samoa my home."

Key Terms:

- **Revival**: Renewed attention to or interest in something.

- **Self-employed**: Earning income directly from one's own business instead of earning a salary or wages from an employer.

Discussion Questions:

- Pua's job is not traditional. She doesn't have a boss, or an office, or a paycheck, but she loves the business she has built! What do you think—would you enjoy being self-employed? Is that something you'd like to try in your life?

Chapter Sixteen

Educational Opportunities for Aspiring Artists and Siapo Makers

In order for art to thrive in American Samoa, we need more young people like Pua and Talanoa who want to learn the traditional art forms and carry on these practices of Samoan culture. If you are interested in pursuing art as your career, there are many educational opportunities in the world for you to explore!

This chapter will walk you through some options for studying art after high school, including pursuing an apprenticeship in American Samoa or studying at one of the universities that helped us conduct the research for this book.

Apprenticeships in American Samoa

If you are an aspiring artist and siapo maker, one option for developing your skills is to become an apprentice. Apprenticeship is a form of learning through mentorship that has been used around the world for centuries.

Instead of taking classes through a college or institution, an apprentice works directly under a master craftsman to learn a specific set of skills. As you've read in previous chapters, artists in American Samoa, such as Su'a Uilisone Fitiao and Reggie Meredith Fitiao, have studied as apprentices to become siapo makers and tattoo masters in addition to their studies in school.

In a master-apprentice learning model, the apprentice learns gradually over time by assisting the master, observing their skills, and then creating their own art.

Becoming an apprentice is a long-term commitment. Artists like Reggie studied with siapo makers for years, and Su'a Uilisone worked for seven years under his master before officially becoming a tufuga ta tatau.

This type of learning is an amazing way to practice the methods of an indigenous art form specific to the Samoan islands. If you hope to someday learn siapo through an apprenticeship, the best place to start is by taking siapo workshops available in American Samoa. Artists like Reggie Meredith Fitiao regularly offer siapo workshops for youth and adults to engage with siapo.

If you are interested in siapo workshops or eventually pursuing an apprenticeship, you can find more information on the Fa'asamoa Arts website.

The American Samoa Community College Fine Arts Department

If you are interested in learning art in a traditional classroom environment, the American Samoa Community College Fine Arts Department offers an Associate of Arts (A.A.) Degree with an Emphasis in Visual Arts ("College, American Samoa Community").

Students who pursue this degree and community members interested in taking a course at ASCC may take classes such as Indigenous Art Forms, Art History, Drawing, and Cultural Anthropology. The Indigenous Art Forms course offers students hands-on experience in siapo making, woodcarving, and other traditional Samoan artforms.

This A.A. degree is fantastic for aspiring artists living in American Samoa who want to learn from local artists and art teachers. Art students at ASCC are often invited to participate in arts-related projects around the island, including mural projects and large siapo projects.

Rhode Island School of Design

The Rhode Island School of Design is one of the most prestigious art schools in the United States. The school offers advanced degrees in textiles and houses several siapo from American Samoa and Samoa in their museum collection.

If you are interested in studying siapo in depth, and exploring the world of textile arts, then RISD is a fantastic option for advanced study. According to the program's information page, "In Textiles, you experiment with new materials, technologies, and techniques to design and create innovative fabric and fine art" ("Textiles").

The Rhode Island School of Design offers a Bachelor of Fine Arts Degree in Textiles and a Master of Fine Arts Degree in Textiles.

University of Oregon

The University of Oregon offers a variety of visual arts degrees with different specialization options. If you are interested in developing skills directly connected to siapo-making, you can earn your Bachelor of Arts degree in Visual Art with a concentration in Fabrics or Drawing and Painting.

In addition to their degree programs, the University of Oregon is also home to a collection of tapa. The University of Oregon Museum of Natural and Cultural History has more than 80 tapa from the Pacific in their collection. They also house barkcloth from other parts of the world, such as Mozambique and Congo (Briggs).

Choosing Where to Study Art and Siapo

Learning from other artists and teachers is the best way to grow as an artist and develop your skills. There are many different paths you can take on your journey to become an artist, and with so many choices, it can be hard to choose what path to take.

If you are interested in applying for higher education as you finish high school, ask yourself these questions:

1.   What kinds of art do you want to make? If you are interested in making siapo, then an apprenticeship or a degree program in textiles or painting could be good options.

2.   What kinds of funding are available? When you are applying to colleges, look into scholarship programs that can help pay for your tuition. For example, the American Samoa Government offers scholarships for students to pursue degrees off-island.

3.   Where do you want to live? If you want, or need, to stay in American Samoa, then look into the options that are available for learning about art and siapo on-island.

No matter your age, now is the time to start dreaming! You can do research, build your portfolio of artwork, and make plans for your future in artistry.

Key Terms:

- **Apprenticeship**: A learning arrangement where one person (the apprentice) learns a craft, trade, or art from another person (the master).

- **Associate of Arts (A.A.)**: A degree earned at a junior college that can normally be completed in two years of full-time study.

- **Bachelor of Arts (B.A.)**: A degree earned by taking courses through a college or university with a focus on studies in the arts and humanities. This degree normally takes four years of full-time study to complete.

- **Scholarship**: An amount of money given to a student by a person, organization, or government as a form of financial aid to pay for education costs.

- **Portfolio**: A selection of a student's work (such as creative work, academic papers, and tests) compiled over a period of time and used for assessing performance, ability, or progress.

Discussion Questions:

- Which option for learning traditional artistic methods interested you the most in this chapter? Why?

- Do you have plans to continue learning after high school through an apprenticeship or college/university? What are your plans and how did you decide what route was best for you?

Finding Evidence of the Maker

Alyssa Rina, Objects Conservator

Alyssa Rina is an objects conservator who has spent the last nine years fixing and caring for objects and cultural materials in museums, historic homes, and universities across the United States. She's currently employed as an objects conservator at the Western Archeological and Conservation Center in Tucson, Arizona.

Before beginning her work in Tucson, Alyssa gained experience working at institutions such as the Philadelphia Museum of Art, the Alaska State Museum, and the American Museum of Natural History, to name a few. At the time of this book's publication, she has seven years of experience working with Indigenous cultural materials, and graduated with her Master of Science in Art Conservation from the

Winterthur/University of Delaware Program in Art Conservation in August 2023.

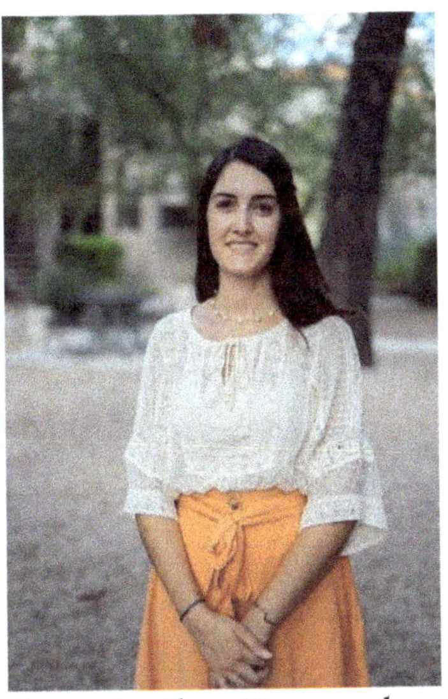

Figure 65: Alyssa Rina, an objects conservator, has spent her career caring for museum collections. Photo by Jesse Michalski, 2022.

Becoming an Art Conservator

Alyssa's path to conservation work began in 2013 when she earned her Bachelor of Fine Arts in Visual and Critical Studies. Her undergraduate degree is in studio arts, rather than art conservation, but the emerging conservator notes that a specific undergraduate degree isn't required to become a conservator.

"The beautiful thing about conservation is that people come to it through different paths and bachelor's degrees," Alyssa says. "People come to conservation with degrees in art history, studio arts, anthropology, archaeology–we even have people who were studying nursing and decided to change their career."

The application process for a graduate program in art conservation is involved. There are only a few such programs in the United States, each of which have similar admissions requirements regarding number of art classes, chemistry classes, material culture-related classes, and work experience of applicants.

Alyssa's degree in studio arts didn't prepare her for all of the application requirements for her master's degree, so she took chemistry classes after work for several years. Beyond the coursework, Alyssa worked hard to gain experience in museums. In the past, the internships and work experience required were often unpaid, but this is beginning to change in the field.

"The field as a whole, in the last five years, has recognized that in order to have more diverse candidates from all walks of life, unpaid internships can't be required," Alyssa says, reflecting on shifts that are shepherding more diversity and inclusion into the field of conservation. These paid internships, called the pre-program phase, give applicants the chance to shadow a conservator and learn more about the field, much like an apprenticeship.

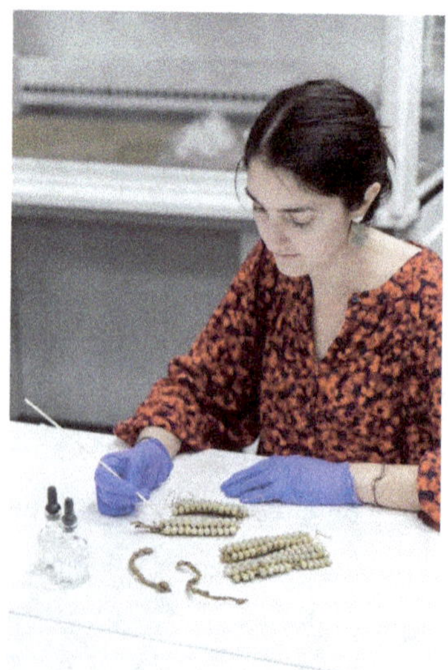

Figure 66: Alyssa cleaning a shell necklace from Papua New Guinea as part of her Object Conservation curriculum. Photo by Evan Krape, 2022.

Finding Evidence of the Maker

The conservation field is broken into several specialties. Alyssa works specifically as an objects conservator, meaning she specializes in working with three dimensional objects. When asked about her favorite parts of being an objects conservator, Alyssa says that the moments that mean the most to her involve the tiniest details. A faint fingerprint, the impression of someone's hand, a piece of hair woven into a basket—these are evidence of the maker, the person who created the object that museum professionals now study.

"I love finding evidence of the maker," Alyssa says. "I've worked on baskets from the Northwest Coast region and found the weaver's hair. We would never remove something like that. Moments like those remind me why I do this work."

In her work at museums, Alyssa has been witness to moments of deep cultural connection. Her work has led her to share spaces with co-curators—cultural practitioners working with museums to inform best practices in conservation and curation. On one occasion, she witnessed an indigenous co-curator who had come to see specific pieces at the museum, only to realize in the moment that the artwork had been created by their ancestor. These are the types of interactions that reiterate how important conservation work really is for maintaining cultural practices and heritage.

Learning from a Siapo Maker

Working with cultural practitioners is a key part of Alyssa's work as a conservator, and this practice is central to her interactions with siapo.

"My experience treating siapo came from my time in my graduate program. I had never come across that kind of material before," Alyssa remembers. On a material level, the methods behind the production of siapo interested her as a student. On a cultural level, she lucky enough to learn about siapo not from a book, but from a siapo maker.

The graduate students studying object conservation at the Winterthur program and their supervising professor, Lara Kaplan, met virtually with Reggie Meredith Fitiao to develop solutions for a piece of barkcloth art they were working to repair. Alyssa's cohort worked with Reggie, Lara, and Winterthur's Paper Conservator and professor, Joan Irving, to stabilize a piece of siapo that had been passed down from the previous cohort of Winterthur graduate students studying object conservation.

"There was this horrible packing tape that was put on the back. Somebody had good intentions, they wanted to hold the siapo together," Alyssa says, remembering the damage that many pieces of tape caused. The cohort before Alyssa's successfully removed the pieces of tape, but the adhesive residues left behind by the tape reacted with the air. They became stiff, incredibly sticky, and impossible to remove safely from the siapo. After many failed attempts to remove the adhesive, the team of students and professors developed a technique to leave the residues in place and cover them. Since this technique is less common in conservation, they all turned to Reggie to make sure this was appropriate for the siapo.

"We came up with a solution that Reggie approved," Alyssa says. "We took pieces of very thin mulberry paper tissue and toned it to match the color of the siapo. Then we coated the paper with a safe adhesive and let that dry. This is called 'pre-coated tissue' and functions like a band-aide. We placed the pre-coated tissue over the old adhesive residue and gently patted it down." The pre-coated paper covered the old residue which was incredibly sticky and added extra support to those fragile areas. Since the tape had been placed on the back of the siapo, the original design was not disrupted by adding the pre-coated tissue.

Working with a cultural practitioner like Reggie provided the group with the knowledge they needed to best treat the damaged siapo. This practice is becoming more common in 21st-century museums when professionals are working with materials that come from contemporary and living indigenous cultures.

"At Winterthur, we asked for Reggie's opinion to see her thoughts on the treatment of siapo," Alyssa explains. "At the Arizona State

Museum, we would work on Navajo and Hopi silver jewelry. In that process, my supervisor worked with Navajo and Hopi jewelry makers to determine how much polishing and treatment we should be doing."

Working directly with a siapo maker allowed the Winterthur conservators to give the best possible treatment to a precious cultural treasure of Samoa. The treatment to stabilize the siapo at Winterthur will be completed by the graduate students in the next cohort and will include continued input from Reggie.

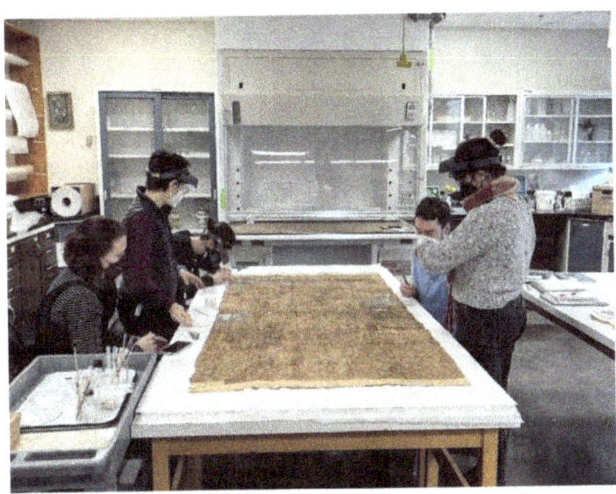

Figure 67: Winterthur/University of Delaware Program in Art Conservation graduate fellows in Object Conservation (from left to right), Katie Shulman, Elle Friedberg, Alyssa Rina, Olav Bjornerud, and Meghan Abercrombie testing treatment options on siapo. Photo by Lara Kaplan.

Thinking Outside the Box

When asked about her advice for young people who are interested in pursuing careers in art conservation and museum studies, Alyssa says that excitement is important.

"Stay excited about art in general, not just fine art. Be excited and play around with making things—try making paper, buy a printmaking kit, start weaving, build something out of wood—anything really. The more you understand how art is created, the easier it can be to figure out how to fix it when it breaks and care for it in the long run," Alyssa advises, thinking back to her undergraduate degree in studio arts and her childhood spent creating and problem-solving whenever she had the chance.

"Remaining creative and thinking outside of the box is a great way to shape your brain for conservation," Alyssa says.

For students in high school, Alyssa recommends reaching out to professionals in the field to learn more about their work and to connect with their local museums and historical societies.

"If you are really interested, reach out to a conservator and start the conversation," she recommends, urging students to connect with museum professionals throughout their schooling as they prepare for their graduate studies.

For conservators, creative thinking and problem solving skills are essential. Focusing on art and science-related undergraduate degrees in college can teach students these skills and prepare them for graduate training in art conservation. However, Alyssa also wants young students to see the benefits of studying a variety of subjects: "Archaeology, anthropology, even studying medicine—learn to problem solve in whatever you choose to study."

Key Terms:

- **Objects conservator**: An art conservator who specializes in the care, restoration, and repair of three-dimensional objects.

- **Material culture**: Tangible objects like tools, crafts, and art works made by a people to define their lives and their culture.

- **Internship**: Supervised, practical work experience completed by someone who is studying within a specific field.

- **Cohort**: In reference to educational experiences, a cohort is a group of scholars who begin and complete a program together.

Discussion Questions:

- Learning from a siapo maker helped Alyssa and her cohort find the best way to care for siapo in their program. But first, they had to ask for help. Do you ask for help from your elders and teachers when you need it? Why or why not?

Chapter Eighteen

Educational Opportunities for Aspiring Museum Professionals

We need more people with the courage to make new art—but we also need people who are passionate about conserving and protecting the art made by past generations. If you are interested in learning how to properly conserve or curate the art of the past, including tapa, then there are certain types of degrees that can put you on the right path.

The following programs are just a few of the options available. There are many opportunities for aspiring museum professionals to learn the necessary skills to preserve the measina (precious things) of American Samoa.

Harvard University

With an interest in becoming an art conservator, collections manager, or museum curator, your first step should be earning a bachelor's degree in a related field. These degrees normally take four years to complete and there are many different schools that offer bachelor's degrees that can help launch your career as a museum professional.

One of these schools is Harvard University, one of the oldest universities in the United States, and one that offers many different degree options for aspiring museum professionals, including:

- Anthropology

- Art, Film, and Visual Studies

- Chemistry

- History of Art and Architecture

Each of these degrees can provide you with the chance to learn the skills needed to work in a museum (Harvard University).

The Winterthur Program, University of Delaware

Earning a master's degree in art conservation is a fantastic next step towards developing your skills and improving your chances of being hired as a conservator by a museum.

The Winterthur/University of Delaware Program in Art Conservation (WUDPAC) is one of the top programs in the United States ("Graduate Programs: Art Conservation"). According to WUDPAC, the students in their three-year program learn:

- Critical thinking and problem solving;

- Communication and leadership;

- Techniques to use in the "ethical treatment of cultural property;"

- And other necessary skills for success in the field.

Students spend the first two years of the program learning to care for, preserve, and restore artifacts and conducting research in Delaware. The third year is spent working under an art conservator at one of WUDPAC's partner institutions.

When applying for a master's program in art conservation at Winterthur/University of Delaware, the application requirements are an undergraduate degree with at least a 2.5 G.P.A., 18 credit hours in material culture studies, 16 credit hours in science, four art classes, and at least 400 hours of conservation experience from internships and past employment at museums.

If you want to someday apply for a master's program like that at Winterthur, then it is a good idea to plan ahead and take the required classes during your time in college.

Earning a master's in art conservation requires a student to dive deep into studying not only the history, but the chemistry of the objects held in museum collections and how those two worlds are deeply interconnected in the field of art conservation.

Internships and Work Experience at Museums

While it's important for future museum professionals to spend time in a classroom, it's also important to gain hands-on experience working in museums. There are paid museum internships available around the United States, but beyond formal internships, you can also pursue volunteer opportunities at museums. At the middle and high school levels there are often opportunities to volunteer with local museums or arts organizations. Volunteering can help give you a better understanding of what museum professionals do and provide you with concrete work experience that can lead to future opportunities.

Key Terms:

- **Museum professional**: A general term used to describe a person who works in museums (including, but not limited to, curators, collections managers, and archivists).

- **Application requirements**: The materials and experiences needed to complete an application for a specific program or position.

Discussion Questions:

- What options listed in this chapter interested you the most? Why?

- Do you have plans to continue learning after high school through an apprenticeship or college/university? What are your plans?

Building a Brighter Future for Siapo

In American Samoa, there are several organizations working to build a brighter future for siapo. These organizations are creating opportunities for young people to learn about this ancient artform and carry it forward for future generations.

Fa'asamoa Arts

Folauga o le Tatau ma laga Aganu'u Fa'asamoa, also known as Fa'asamoa Arts, is a nonprofit organization in Leone, American Samoa. Su'a Uilisone Fitiao and Reggie Meredith Fitiao started their nonprofit to "breathe new life" into traditional Samoan art forms like siapo, with the goal of bringing these artforms into the future.

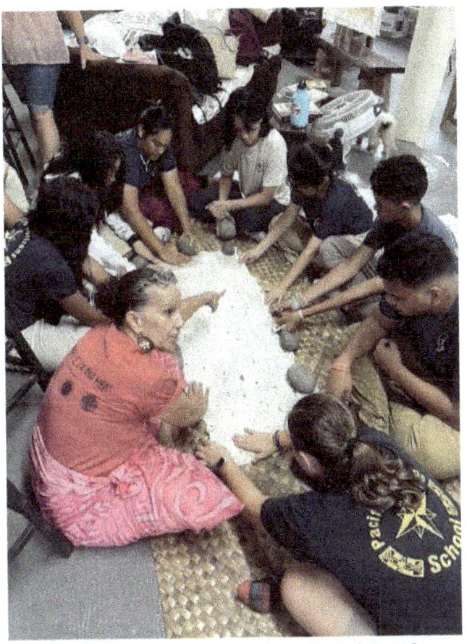

Figure 68: Reggie teaches local students (Pacific Horizons School) how to process bark to create cloth. Photo by Mary Anne Peck.

Fa'asamoa Arts offers youth siapo workshops, partners with the Jean P. Haydon Museum to create and curate siapo exhibits, and works to build connections between American Samoa and museums and universities around the world.

Jean P. Haydon Museum

The Museum of American Samoa was created in 1970, and it opened its doors in the village of Fagatogo on Flag Day in 1973. Later renamed the Jean P. Haydon Museum, the current building houses more than 650 objects of cultural and historic significance. The collection includes several pieces of siapo (Jean P. Haydon Museum).

The Jean P. Haydon Museum Board of Trustees oversees the facility and is appointed by the Governor of American Samoa. Reggie Meredith Fitiao currently works with the museum as a board member and siapo maker to create siapo-focused displays and activities for visitors, students, and tourists.

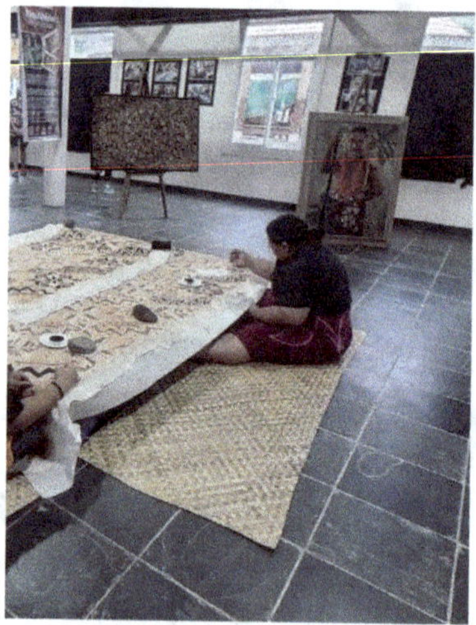

Figure 69: Jean P. Haydon Museum offers public outreach events, including events for siapo making. Photo provided by Jean P. Haydon Museum.

Amerika Samoa Humanities Council

The Amerika Samoa Humanities Council has served the island of American Samoa for 25 years, providing funding to local nonprofit organizations and sponsoring research projects and community programs ("Talofa and Welcome!"). They are an affiliate of the National Endowment for the Humanities.

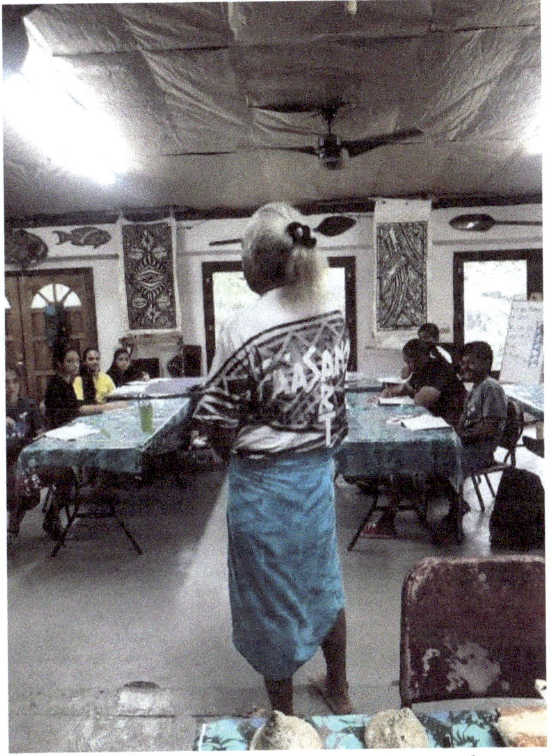

Figure 70: Su'a Uilisone instructs students in the 2021 Siapo Workshops funded by Amerika Samoa Humanities Council. Photo by Fynn Peck.

American Samoa Community College Fine Arts Department

The American Samoa Community College Fine Arts Department offers classes in music, theater, and visual arts, with Associate of Arts degrees in music and visual arts. The goal of the ASCC Fine Arts Department is to cultivate creative expression and encourage students to study the historical and cultural impact of the arts.

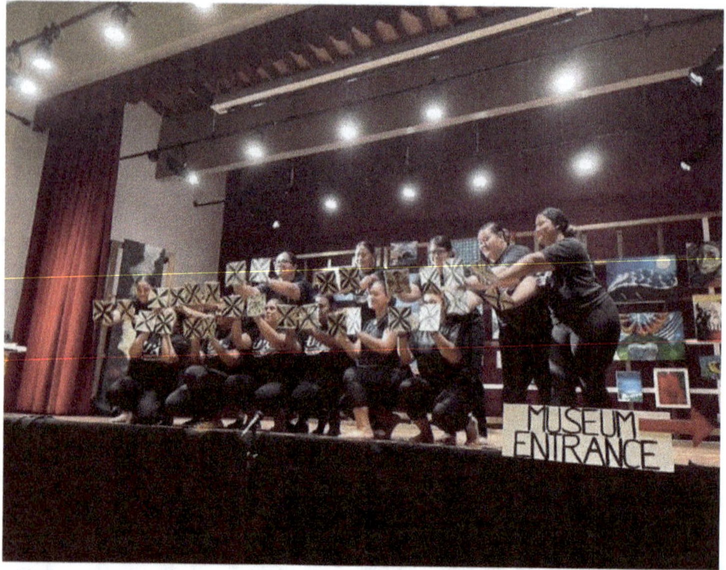

Figure 71: Students at ASCC performing in a show inspired by siapo and museum studies. Photo by Mary Anne Peck.

Getting Involved

There are many groups of passionate people in American Samoa who are building a better future for the arts and for siapo on our island.

If you are interested in getting involved in the arts in American Samoa, you can:

- Participate in siapo workshops with Fa'asamoa Arts.

- Visit our local museum and learn about the siapo and other artifacts in their collection.

- Attend events like shows and community events hosted by the ASCC Fine Arts Department, or enroll in a fine arts class to get more hands-on experience.

- Connect with the projects that the Amerika Samoa Humanities Council sponsors each year.

Let's Build a Brighter Future for Siapo

Siapo has existed for generations, passed down from teacher to student for centuries. The number of siapo makers in American Samoa has shrunk with time, but we have a chance today to do our part to build a brighter future for siapo.

The u'a takes care of the people of Samoa, and this care should be returned wholeheartedly. By learning about siapo, speaking with siapo makers, and supporting local museums and artists, you can be a part of a revitalization of siapo-making in American Samoa.

E teu lava e le u'a ana mea.

Key Terms:

- **Humanities**: Areas of study (such as philosophy, arts, or languages) that focus on human ideas, creations, and concerns, instead of natural processes (such as the sciences).

- **Revitalization**: The act of giving new life or rigor to something.

- **Fine Arts**: Art (such as painting, sculpture, and architecture) concerned primarily with the creation of beautiful objects.

Discussion Questions:

- The siapo makers of American Samoa have worked for generations to move siapo forward and teach the next generation. What can you do to help their efforts?

- E teu lava e le u'a ana mea. The u'a takes care of its own. After reading this book, what do you believe this proverb means?

GLOSSARY OF KEY TERMS

The following definitions are informed by *Encyclopedia Britannica*, *Merriam-Webster Dictionary*, and the knowledge of the museum professionals and siapo makers featured in *Siapo: Yesterday, Today, and Tomorrow*.

CHAPTER 1: E TEU LAVA E LE U'A ANA MEA

- **U'a**: The Samoan term for barkcloth made from the paper mulberry tree.

- **Siapo**: U'a that is decorated with natural dyes using Samoan ancestral patterns.

- **Art conservation**: The maintenance and preservation of works of art and their protection from future damage and deterioration.

- **Mana**: Among the people of the Pacific, mana describes a supernatural force or spiritual power that people, places, and objects can have.

- **Malaga**: The Samoan term for a journey, specifically a journey taken with other people.

CHAPTER 2: WHAT IS BARKCLOTH?

- **Barkcloth**: A fabric made from the inner bark of trees. Barkcloth making involves scraping and beating the bark, then separating the fibers to create sheets of flexible cloth.

- **Bast**: A strong fiber that lays under the rough outer bark of trees. The bast is used by many cultures to create cords, matts, and fabric.

- **Lacebark**: Barkcloth made in Jamaica by teasing the fibers of the inner bark of the lagetto tree.

- **Ngatu**: Barkcloth made in the traditions of the Kingdom of Tonga.

- **Hiapo**: The paper mulberry tree and the barkcloth derived from the tree are both referred to as "hiapo" in the Tongan language.

- **Kapa**: Barkcloth made in the traditions of the Hawaiian people.

- **Masi**: Barkcloth made in the traditions of the Fijian people.

CHAPTER 3: A BRIEF HISTORY OF TAPA

- **Tapa**: A "universal" term for decorated barkcloth made throughout the Pacific.

- ***Broussonetia papyrifera***: The scientific name for paper mulberry, called u'a in Samoa.

- **Anthropologist**: An expert in anthropology, the study of humanity, ranging from the evolution of Homo sapiens to the societies and cultures that have developed throughout human history.

- **Historian**: An expert who studies history, the study of the events through the examination of source materials and records.

- **Botanist**: An expert in botany, a type of biology that focuses on the study of plants.

- **Prehistoric**: An adjective describing something that existed in times before written history.

- **I'e**: A wooden mallet used to sasa le u'a, or beat the bark of the paper mulberry tree to create barkcloth.

- **Austronesian language family**: A family of languages spoken in South Asia and the Central and South Pacific regions. The Austronesian language family is the largest in the world with 1,200 members, including one-fifth of the world's languages.

- **Commensal species/Canoe plants**: Plants (and some animals) that were carried by the people of the Pacific to each new island over years of exploration and settlement.

- **Lapita**: Some researchers agree that the Lapita were the original settlers of the Pacific, including Melanesia, large portions of Polynesia, and sections of Micronesia. They navigated the sea to settle the Pacific islands, arriving in western Polynesia (including Samoa) by 1000 BCE.

- **Tulafale**: A Samoan senior orator who is knowledgeable in the oral history of the Samoan islands.

CHAPTER 4: A REBIRTH OF SIAPO, MARY J. PRITCHARD

- **Fa'asamoa**: The Samoan way of life.

CHAPTER 5: LEADING LEONE'S SIAPOMAKERS, KOLONE LEOSO AND TUI'ULI LEOSO

- **Siapo mamanu**: The freehand style of Samoan siapo.

- **Fale**: The Samoan term for house, an open air building that historically provided shelter for the Samoan people. Currently, fales may be used as meeting houses for families, special events, living quarters, village council meetings, and more.

- **Siapo tasiga** (also known as "**siapo elei**"): The rubbing method of Samoan siapo.

- **Paogo**: A pandanus key. Siapo makers trim the paogo to use as a natural brush for the application of dyes.

- **O'a**: The brown dye used by siapo makers, created using the *Bischofia javanica*.

- **Lama**: The black dye used by siapo makers, created using the candlenut tree, *Aleurites molucannus*.

- **Loa**: The red dye used by siapo makers, created using *Bixa orellana*.

- **Ago**: The yellow dye used by siapo makers, created using *Curcuma longa*.

CHAPTER 6: CARING FOR THE SIAPO OF YESTERDAY, MICHELE AUSTIN-DENNEHY

- **Documentation**: Museum professionals keep accurate records of photographs and information about collections through documentation efforts. Through documentation, museums are able to provide the fullest possible history of each object.

- **Source communities**: The communities that created the objects currently housed in museums around the world. (Ex: Samoa is a source community for many of the tapa housed at the Field Museum of Chicago.)

- **Culturally-appropriate**: Practices, in conservation and other fields, that respect the traditions, beliefs, and preferences of source communities.

- **Cultural practitioners**: Artists and craftsmen with specific knowledge of the ancestral practices of their community.

- **Stabilization**: Practices used by museum professionals, such as conservators, with the purpose of limiting further deterioration of historical objects.

CHAPTER 7: UNDERSTANDING SIAPO AT A MATERIAL LEVEL

- **Sae u'a**: Stripping the bark from the paper mulberry tree.

- **Vavalu**: Scraping the inner bark of the paper mulberry tree to remove debris.

- **Sasa le u'a**: Beating the inner bark of the paper mulberry tree with an i'e (wooden mallet) to create barkcloth.

- **Upeti**: A carved wooden board used to create siapo tasiga. Historically, upeti have also been sewn using materials such as pandanus.

- ***Bischofia javanica***: Also known as the "blood tree," the bark of this tree is scraped and collected for the creation of o'a, the brown dye for siapo.

- **Ipu lama**: A shell used to collect the soot of a burning candlenut for the purpose of creating the lama, the black dye for siapo.

- ***Bixa orellana:*** Also known as the "lipstick tree," the seeds of this tree are collected for the creation of the loa, the red dye for siapo.

- **Samaga**: A ceremonial blessing for a new pe'a or malu, the traditional tattoos of the Samoan islands.

CHAPTER 8: MAMANU: A VISUAL RECORD OF SAMOAN LIFE

- **Mamanu**: The motifs and patterns used in Samoan siapo.

- **Fa'a ali'ao**: The siapo motif that represents the trochus shell and the Samoan people's connection to the ocean.

- **Fa'a anufe**: The siapo motif that represents the worm and the ancestral knowledge of the earth and agriculture.

- **Fa'a gogo**: The siapo motif that represents birds and the navigational practices of Samoans and the people of the Pacific.

- **Fa'a atualoa**: The siapo motif that represents the centipede and the resilience required to overcome hardship and pain.

CHAPTER 9: A STEWARD OF SIAPO, REGGIE MEREDITH FITIAO

- **Measina**: The precious things of Samoa.

- **Palagi**: The Samoan term for a non-Samoan person.

- **Master of Fine Arts**: A high-level degree that artists, writers, musicians, and actors may earn. This degree is considered the terminal degree, or highest possible degree, that one can pursue in the arts.

- **Terminal degree**: A degree that is the highest level of study in a specific field.

- **Nonprofit organization**: A business not conducted or maintained for the purpose of making a profit.

- **Aiga**: The Samoan term for family.

- **Afakasi**: To be half-Samoan and half-non-Samoan. A general term used in Samoa to describe a person of mixed race.

CHAPTER 10: A MASTER OF MANY ART FORMS, SU'A UILISONE FITIAO

- **Tufuga ta tatau**: A master of the ancestral artform of Samoan tatau. A tufuga must train for several years under the guidance of a master to earn their title.

- **Wayfinding**: A practice of navigation and sailing in the tradition of the Samoan people.

- **Apprentice**: One who is learning by practical experience under skilled workers of a trade, art, or calling.

CHAPTER 11: BRINGING SIAPO TO NEW MEDIUMS, NICHOLAS KING

- **Commission**: A formal request to produce something (especially an artistic work) in exchange for payment from a specific client.

- **Innovation**: A new idea, method, or device. The introduction of something new.

CHAPTER 12: STUDYING SIAPO IN MUSEUMS

- **Polymer exterior varnish**: A waterproof, UV-resistant, clear coating that can be used as a sealant.

- **Infrared**: When used in reference to imaging, infrared describes images that capture light outside the visible spectrum at its red end.

- **Ultraviolet**: When used in reference to imaging, ultraviolet describes images that capture light outside the visible spectrum at its violet end.

- **Co-curation**: A practice in modern museums that involves the inclusion of source communities and outside experts in the curatorial process and creation of exhibits.

CHAPTER 13: CO-CURATION WITH CULTURAL PRACTIONERS, CHRISTOPHER PHILIP

- **Collections manager**: A museum professional who manages the items in the collection through preventative conservation and community access.

- **Museum studies**: The science or profession of museum organization and management.

- **Ethnomusicology**: The study of music from around the world, including the study of musical instruments.

- **Curator**: A person who oversees or manages a place (such as a museum) that offers exhibits.

- **Storage boxes/mounts**: Items built to better store and display museum collections.

- **Preventative conservation**: The act of preventing further deterioration by controlling the storage environment of museum objects.

- **Archival materials**: Materials such as acid-free paper and storage containers that help conservators to safely store fragile materials.

CHAPTER 14: MAKING ART THAT MOVES THE AUDIENCE, TALANOA LAGAFUAINA

- **Surrealism**: A movement in the arts that focuses on positive expression and the defiance of reality and reason. It came about initially as a reaction to the horrors of World Wars I and II (1914-1945). Artists associated with this period include Salvador Dali and Frida Kahlo.

- **Ka'a**: A Samoan term for time spent physically escaping from daily responsibilities or mentally escaping from reality.

- **Fa'alavelave**: Situations that require the attention of the family (such as a funeral).

CHAPTER 15: STRENGTHENING CULTURAL CONNECTION THROUGH ART, PUA TOFAEONO

- **Revival**: Renewed attention to or interest in something.

- **Self-employed**: Earning income directly from one's own business instead of earning a salary or wages from an employer.

CHAPTER 16: EDUCATIONAL OPPORTUNITIES FOR ASPIRING ARTISTS

- **Apprenticeship**: A learning arrangement where one person (the apprentice) learns a craft, trade, or art from another person (the master).

- **Associate of Arts (A.A.)**: A degree earned at a junior college that can normally be completed in two years of full-time study.

- **Bachelor of Arts (B.A.)**: A degree earned by taking courses through a college or university with a focus on studies in the arts and humanities. This degree normally takes four years of full-time study to complete.

- **Scholarship**: An amount of money given to a student by a person, organization, or government as a form of financial aid to pay for education.

- **Portfolio**: A selection of a student's work (such as creative work, academic papers, and tests) compiled over a period of time and used for assessing performance or progress.

CHAPTER 17: FINDING EVIDENCE OF THE MAKER, ALYSSA RINA

- **Objects conservator**: An art conservator who specializes in the care, restoration, and repair of three-dimensional objects.

- **Material culture**: Tangible objects like tools, crafts, and art works made by a people to define their lives and their culture.

- **Internship**: Supervised, practical work experience completed by someone who is studying within a specific field.

- **Cohort**: In reference to educational experiences, a cohort is a group of scholars who begin and complete a program together.

CHAPTER 18: EDUCATIONAL OPPORTUNITIES FOR ASPIRING CONSERVATORS

- **Museum professional**: A general term used to describe a person who works in museums(including, but not limited to, curators, collections managers, and archivists).

- **Application requirements**: The materials and experiences needed to complete an application for a specific program or position.

CHAPTER 19: BUILDING A BRIGHTER FUTURE FOR SIAPO

- **Humanities**: Areas of study (such as philosophy, arts, or languages) that focus on human ideas, creations, and concerns, instead of natural processes (such as the sciences).

- **Revitalization**: The act of giving new life or rigor to something.

- **Fine Arts**: Art (such as painting, sculpture, and architecture) concerned primarily with the creation of beautiful objects.

DISCUSSION QUESTIONS

The following discussion questions are listed at the end of each chapter. They can be used to guide conversations with classmates, friends, and family as you read this book.

CHAPTER 1: E TEU LAVA E LE U'A ANA MEA

- E teu lava e le u'a ana mea. The u'a takes care of its own. What does this proverb mean to you? Do you believe that a piece of art can carry spiritual power?

- How can learning about the lives and art of siapo makers and artists help you to learn more about Samoan culture?

- If you have heard about siapo before reading this book, what do you already know? Share your knowledge with the group!

CHAPTER 2: WHAT IS BARKCLOTH?

- Which form of barkcloth discussed in this chapter interests you the most? Why?

- How does barkcloth art unify the Pacific?

CHAPTER 3: A BRIEF HISTORY OF TAPA

- Why is u'a (paper mulberry) studied by scientists? What can they learn from u'a?

- Why would Pacific navigators include paper mulberry with their canoe plants?

CHAPTER 4: A REBIRTH OF SIAPO, MARY J. PRITCHARD

- What lesson can be learned from Mary Pritchard's failure the first time she tried to make her own siapo? How can failure be a good thing?

- The women of Leone worked together to create each siapo, and siapo artists today still utilize this group method for some projects. How does working as a group add meaning to the siapo making process?

CHAPTER 5: LEADING LEONE'S SIAPOMAKERS, KOLONE LEOSO AND TUI'ULI LEOSO

- Kolone Leoso made a difference by teaching other people

and spreading her passion for art throughout her village and her island. What is something you are passionate about that you could teach to the people around you?

- Without siapo makers like Kolone and Tui'uli, siapo may have been lost in American Samoa in the years after World War II. This is just one example of how great an impact a teacher can have. Share about a time when a teacher changed your life for the better.

CHAPTER 6: CARING FOR THE SIAPO OFYES-TERDAY, MICHELE AUSTIN-DENNEHY

- Art conservation has changed over the years–from a scientific focus to a collaborative process with source communities. What do you think of these changes?

- Conservators, scientists, botanists, archivists, historians, and curators—these are just some of the experts that help make art conservation possible. Which one is most interesting to you and why?

CHAPTER 7: UNDERSTANDING SIAPO AT A MATERIAL LEVEL

- If you have seen siapo before at home, in a museum, or at a market, are you surprised to learn the amount of work that it takes to prepare the materials? What did you think the process was before reading this chapter?

- Siapo makers have a strong connection with the earth and the resources that make siapo possible. What parts of nature do you strongly connect with in your life?

CHAPTER 8: MAMANU: A VISUAL RECORD OF SAMOAN LIFE

- The mamanu are one way that previous generations shared their knowledge. What is something you have learned from a previous generation through art or stories?

- The fa'a atualoa represents hardship and pain, but also the strength and resilience it takes to overcome that pain. Can you remember a time when you or a loved one was resilient in the face of hardship?

CHAPTER 9: A STEWARD OF SIAPO, REGGIE MEREDITH FITIAO

- Every person's identity is complex. We are a combination of the people who came before us, the cultures we inhabit, the life events we experience, and the beliefs that shape our decisions. Reggie has embraced her identity as a siapo maker *and* an artist *and* a teacher. These pieces all combine to make Reggie who she is. Try to list out some of the important parts of who you are! What are the puzzle pieces that create your identity?

- The people in our lives help to sculpt who we are—try to list some of the elders, teachers, and family members who have impacted you.

CHAPTER 10: A MASTER OF MANY ART FORMS, SU'A UILISONE FITIAO

- Su'a Uilisone took extra steps to receive a blessing from his teacher before using tatau motifs in his siapo. These extra steps are just one way that he shows respect for the masters who came before him. What are some ways that you can show respect and acknowledge the people who came before you?

- Based on what you read in Su'a Uilisone's chapter—what do you think the differences are between tatau motifs and siapo motifs?

CHAPTER 11: BRINGING SIAPO TO NEW MEDIUMS, NICHOLAS KING

- Nick uses siapo motifs to create a wide range of art. His creativity and innovation has led to surprising and memorable experiences. What do you think are the benefits of creativity?

- Nick and his teachers all shared a simple truth: talent isn't enough, you have to put in the time and effort to create art. Do you agree with their opinion?

CHAPTER 12: STUDYING SIAPO IN MUSEUMS

- There are many ways siapo is studied in museums. What method of study interested you most in this chapter? Photography, digital archives, hands-on study?

CHAPTER 13: CO-CURATION WITH CULTURAL PRACTIONERS, CHRISTOPHER PHILIP

- Co-curation involves collaboration between museums and source communities. How do these two groups work together to care for collections?

CHAPTER 14: MAKING ART THAT MOVES THE AUDIENCE, TALANOA LAGAFUAINA

- Talanoa finds inspiration in the fa'alavelave (specifically the funeral traditions) of Samoa. In what other ways can we find inspiration in grief, sadness, etc.?

- What role should young people play in the future of siapo?

CHAPTER 15: STRENGTHENING CULTURAL CONNECTION THROUGH ART, PUA TOFAEONO

- Pua's job is not traditional. She doesn't have a boss, or an office, or a paycheck, but she loves the business she has built! What do you think—would you enjoy being self-employed? Is that something you'd like to try in your life?

CHAPTER 16: EDUCATIONAL OPPORTUNITIES FOR ASPIRING ARTISTS

- Which option for learning traditional artistic methods interested you the most in this chapter? Why?

- Do you have plans to continue learning after high school through an apprenticeship or college/university? What are your plans and how did you decide what route was best for you?

CHAPTER 17: FINDING EVIDENCE OF THE MAKER, ALYSSA RINA

- Learning from a siapo maker helped Alyssa and her cohort find the best way to care for siapo in their program. But first, they had to ask for help. Do you ask for help from your elders and teachers when you need it? Why or why not?

CHAPTER 18: EDUCATIONAL OPPORTUNITIES FOR ASPIRING CONSERVATORS

- What options listed in this chapter interested you the most?

Why?

- Do you have plans to continue learning after high school through an apprenticeship or college/university? What are your plans?

CHAPTER 19: BUILDING A BRIGHTER FUTURE FOR SIAPO

- The siapo makers of American Samoa have worked for generations to move siapo forward and teach the next generation. What can you do to help their efforts?

- E teu lava e le u'a ana mea. The u'a takes care of its own. After reading this book, what do you believe that this proverb means?

WORKS CITED

T he following citations are arranged by order of appearance within each chapter.

CHAPTER 1: E TEU LAVA E LE U'A ANA MEA

Peck, Mary Anne. "Conversation with Su'a Uilisone Fitiao and Regina Meredith Fitiao." Aug. 2023.

CHAPTER 2: WHAT IS BARKCLOTH?

"The Ancient Craft of Barkcloth across the World." *National Museums Scotland*, www.nms.ac.uk/explore-our-collections/stories/global-arts-cultures-and-design/understanding-barkcloth-at-national-museums-scotland/.

Walusimbi, J. K. "UNESCO - Barkcloth Making in Uganda." *Intangible Cultural Heritage*, United Nations Education, Scientific and Cultural Organization, 2008,ich.unesco.org/en/RL/barkcloth-making-in-uganda-00139.

Buckridge, Steeve O. "African Lace-Bark in the Caribbean: The Construction of Race, Class, and Gender." *Bloomsbury Academic*, Bloomsbury Publishing, 14 July 2016, www.bloomsbury.com/us/african-lacebark-in-the-caribbean-9781472569318/.

"Robe: Japan (Ainu)." *The Metropolitan Museum of Art*, Gift of John B. Elliott through the Mercer Trust, 1999,2000, www.metmuseum.org/art/collection/search/53902.

Aragon, Lorraine V. "Barkcloth Production in Central Sulawesi." *Expedition Magazine*, Penn Museum, 1990, www.penn.museum/sites/expedition/barkcloth-production-in-central-sulawesi/.

Awatea, Tai. "Ngatu, Tapa." *Collections Online - Museum of New Zealand Te Papa Tongarewa*, 2007, collections.tepapa.govt.nz/topic/1098#:~:text=Ngatu%20is%20made%20from%20the,the%20inner%20and%20outer%20bark.

"Kapa." *National Parks Service*, U.S. Department of the Interior, www.nps.gov/hale/learn/historyculture/kapa.htm. Accessed 5 Nov. 2024.

"Masi (Tapa Cloth) ." *Museum of New Zealand Te Papa Tongarewa*, Gift of the Wellcome Museum, 1952,collections.tepapa.govt.nz/object/155316.

CHAPTER 3: A BRIEF HISTORY OF TAPA

Seelenfreund , Daniela, et al. *Paper Mulberry (Broussonetia Papyrifera) as a Commensal Model for Human Mobility in Oceania: Anthropological, Botanical and Genetic Considerations*, New Zealand Journal of Botany, Jan. 2011, www.researchgate.net/publication/220042284_Paper_mulberry_Broussonetia_papyrifera_as_a_commensal_model_for_human_ mobility_in_Oceania_Anthropological_botanical_and_genetic_considerations.

Li, Dawei, et al. "The Oldest Bark Cloth Beater in Southern China (Dingmo, Bubing Basin, Guangxi)." *Quaternary International, Volume 345*, Pergamon, 19 July 2014, www.sciencedirect.com/science/article/abs/pii/S1040618214004364.

"Austronesian Languages." *Encyclopædia Britannica*, Encyclopædia Britannica, inc., 29 Aug. 2024, www.britannica.com/topic/Austronesian-languages.

Ko, Albert Min-Shan, et al. "Early Austronesians: Into and out of Taiwan." *American Journal of Human Genetics*, U.S. National Library of Medicine, 6 Mar. 2014,pmc.ncbi.nlm.nih.gov/articles/PMC3951936/#:~:text=Bayesian%20phylogenetic%20analysis%20allows%20us,Asia%2C%20Madagascar%2C%20and%20Oceania.

Olivares, Gabriela, et al. "Human Mediated Translocation of Pacific Paper Mulberry [Broussonetia Papyrifera (L.)L'Hér. Ex Vent. (Moraceae)]: Genetic Evidence of Dispersal Routes in Remote Oceania." *PloS One*, U.S. National Library of Medicine, 19 June 2019, www.ncbi.nlm.nih.gov/pmc/articles/PMC6583976/.

Matisoo-Smith, Elizabeth A. "Tracking Austronesian Expansion into the Pacific via the Paper Mulberry Plant." *Proceedings of the National Academy of Sciences of the United States of America*, 23Oct. 2015, www.pnas.org/doi/10.1073/pnas.1518576112.

"Early Samoa: History: Samoa Travel Guide: Pacific Island." *History | Samoa Travel Guide | Pacific Island*, Samoa Tourism Authority, www.samoa.travel/discover/our-history/early-samoa/.

"Lapita Culture." *Encyclopædia Britannica*, Encyclopædia Britannica, inc., www.britannica.com/topic/Lapita-culture. Accessed 24 Oct. 2024.

Pritchard, Mary J. *Siapo: Bark Cloth Art of Samoa*. Council on Culture, Arts, and Humanities, 1984.

About Fiji - History, Fiji High Commission to the United Kingdom, www.fijihighcommission.org.uk/about_1.html. Accessed 24 Oct. 2024.

CHAPTER 4: A REBIRTH OF SIAPO, MARY J. PRITCHARD

Pritchard, Mary J. *Siapo: Bark Cloth Art of Samoa*. Council on Culture, Arts, and Humanities, 1984.

CHAPTER 5: LEADING LEONE'S SIAPO MAKERS, KOLONE LEOSO AND TUI'ULI LEOSO

Pritchard, Mary J. *Siapo: Bark Cloth Art of Samoa*. Council on Culture, Arts, and Humanities, 1984.

CHAPTER 6: CARING FOR THE SIAPO OF YESTERDAY, MICHELE AUSTIN-DENNEHY

Peck, Mary Anne. "Conversation with Michele Austin-Dennehy." 5 Oct. 2023.

Meredith Fitiao, Regina A. "Making Siapo in Leone Today." *Digital Commons at University of Nebraska-Lincoln*, Textile Society of America Symposium Proceedings, 2020, digitalcommons.unl.edu/cgi/viewcontent.cgi?article=1379&context=tsaconf.

CHAPTER 7: UNDERSTANDING SIAPO AT A MATERIAL LEVEL

Peck, Mary Anne. "Conversation with Su'a Uilisone Fitiao and Reggie Meredith Fitiao" 5 Oct. 2023.

CHAPTER 8: MAMANU: A VISUAL RECORD OF SAMOAN LIFE

Peck, Mary Anne. "Conversation with Su'a Uilisone Fitiao and Reggie Meredith Fitiao" 5 Oct. 2023.

Shapiro, Craig H., and Julie S. Field. "The Function of Prehistoric Agricultural Systems in Samoa." *Sustainability in Ancient Island Societies*, 16 Apr. 2024, pp. 142–173,https://doi.org/10.5744/flo rida/9780813069975.003.0006.

CHAPTER 9: A STEWARD OF SIAPO, REGGIE MEREDITH FITIAO

Peck, Mary Anne. "Conversation with Regina Meredith Fitiao." Aug. 2023.

CHAPTER 10: A MASTER OF MANY ART FORMS, SU'A UILISONE FITIAO

Peck, Mary Anne. "Conversation with Su'a Uilisone Fitiao." Aug. 2023.

CHAPTER 11: BRINGING SIAPO TO NEW MEDIUMS, NICHOLAS KING

Peck, Mary Anne. "Conversation with Nicholas F. King Jr." Oct. 2023.

CHAPTER 12: STUDYING SIAPO IN MUSEUMS

Bradley, Kimberly. "Why Museums Hide Masterpieces Away." *BBC News*, BBC, 24 Feb. 2022, www.bbc.com/culture/article/201501 23-7-masterpieces-you-cant-see.

"Care Guidelines-Tapa." *Tapa: Situating Pacific Bark Cloth in Time and Place*, University of Glasgow, Aug.2020,tapa.gla.ac.uk/care-guidelines/#:~:text=Barclot h%20in%20the%20Pacific,supple%20while%20not%20in%20use.

"Tapa Cloths from the Peabody Museum Treated & Photographed IPCH Labs." *Institute for the Preservation of Cultural Heritage*, Yale University, 10 Sept. 2015,ipch.yale.edu/news-events/tapa-cl oths-peabody-museum-treated-photographed-ipch-labs.

CHAPTER 13: CO-CURATION WITH CULTUR-AL PRACTIONERS, CHRISTOPHER PHILIP

Peck, Mary Anne. "Conversation with Christopher Philipp" Sept. 2023.

CHAPTER 14: MAKING ART THAT MOVES THE AUDIENCE, TALANOA LAGAFUAINA

Peck, Mary Anne. "Conversation with Talanoa Lagafuaina." Sept. 2023.

CHAPTER 15: STRENGTHENING CULTURAL CONNECTION THROUGH ART, PUA TOFAEONO

Peck, Mary Anne. "Conversation with Pua Tofaeono." Sept. 2023.

CHAPTER 16: EDUCATIONAL OPPORTUNITIES FOR ASPIRING ARTISTS

College, American Samoa Community." Associate of Arts Degree with an Emphasis in Visual Arts." *AA with an Emphasis in Visual Arts* , American Samoa Community College,www.amsamoa.edu /academicprograms/aavisualart.html. Accessed 5 Nov. 2024.

"Textiles." *RISD*, Rhode Island School of Design, www.risd.edu/ac ademics/textiles.

Briggs, Lexie. "Samoan Researchers Visit UO to See Its Collection of Tapa Cloth." *Oregon News*, University of Oregon, 27 July 2022,around.uoregon.edu/content/samoan-researchers-visit -uo-see-its-collection-tapa-cloth.

CHAPTER 17: FINDING EVIDENCE OF THE MAKER, ALYSSA RINA

Peck, Mary Anne. "Conversation with Alyssa Rina" Sept. 2023.

CHAPTER 18: EDUCATIONAL OPPORTUNI-
TIES FOR ASPIRING CONSERVATORS

Harvard University. "Programs Archive." *Harvard University*, www
.harvard.edu/programs/. Accessed 5 Nov. 2024.

"Graduate Programs: Art Conservation: College of Arts & Sciences:
University of Delaware." *Art Conservation |College of Arts & Sci-
ences | University of Delaware*, www.artcons.udel.edu/masters
/graduate-admissions/admissions-requirements. Accessed 5 Nov.
2024.

CHAPTER 19: BUILDING A BRIGHTER FU-
TURE FOR SIAPO

Jean P Haydon Museum, 30 July 2021, haydonmuseumamericansa
moa.org/.

"Talofa and Welcome!" *AMERIKA SAMOAHUMANITIES
COUNCIL*, 3 Oct. 2023, www.ashcouncil.org/.

"National Endowment for the Humanities." *The National Endowment For The Humanities*, 21 Oct. 2024, www.neh.gov/.

About the Researchers

This book exists because of the expertise of Su'a Uilisone Fitiao and Reggie Meredith Fitiao. Through their nonprofit, Folauga o le Tatau ma laga Aganu'u Fa'asamoa (Fa'asamoa Arts), and funding provided by the Amerika Samoa Humanities Council, we were able to plan a month-long trip that took us across the United States to study siapo in museums and universities.

Su'a Uilisone and Reggie's research and practical knowledge in siapo-making and art conservation made that trip possible, and therefore made this book possible. Information about their studio work and arts advocacy can be found at faasamoaarts.com.

SU'A UILISONE FITIAO

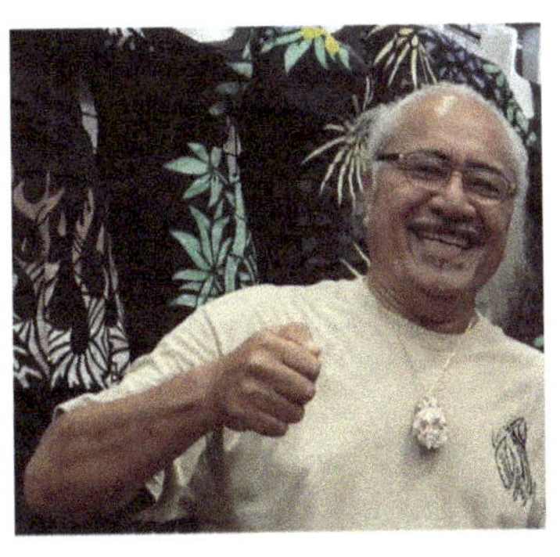

SU'A UILISONE FITIAO is a Tufuga Ta Tatau, wood carver, and siapo maker. Su'a Uilisone's family moved to American Samoa in 1969. He learned the traditional form of painting called siapo in the late 1970s from the late Mary J. Pritchard, who serves as a key inspiration for him. Su'a Uilisone is now a Tufuga ta Tatau, a traditional Samoan Tattoo master, after working with Su'a Lafaele Suluape for almost seven years as his apprentice. He embraces and helps to manage the ancestral and sacred art forms of tatau and siapo, working to ensure that these unique and meaningful parts of Samoan culture last for generations.

REGINA MEREDITH FITIAO

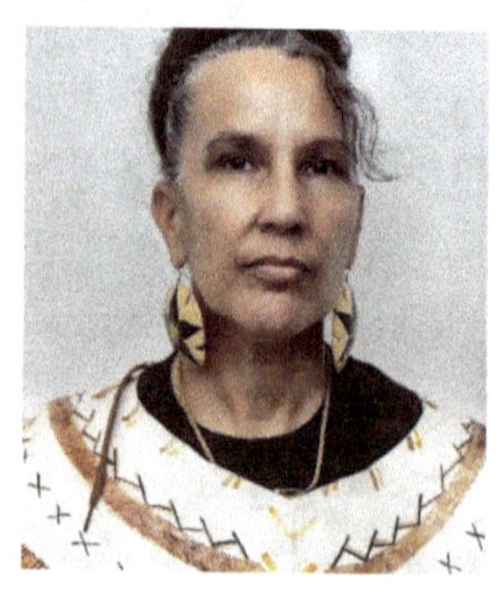

REGINA (REGGIE) MEREDITH FITIAO is a Professor of the Arts, both contemporary and traditional. She is a fourth generation siapo maker who acknowledges her great-grandmother Lemeana'i Saiselu Tuimalealiifano Meredith as one of the women who made siapo in Leone. She credits her knowledge of siapo-making to the teachings of Auntie Mary J. Pritchard. Working with her mother and Aunties Marylyn and Adeline for many years has inspired her to work collaboratively while continuing to pursue an individual style of siapo. With all of the strong women who have embraced her in the richness of siapo, Meredith intends to perpetuate the art form in the rooted foundation that was set for her to the next generation.

ACKNOWLEDGEMENTS

Fa'afetai tele lava to all of the people who helped bring this book into the world.

I'd like to start by saying thank you to my readers–the students and teachers of American Samoa and beyond who are making an effort to learn about siapo. This book is for you.

Thank you to the Amerika Samoa Humanities Council and the National Endowment for the Humanities for funding the research trip that led to the creation of this book and for supporting the Fa'asamoa Arts nonprofit organization since its creation.

Thank you to the museums and universities that welcomed Su'a Uilisone, Reggie, and myself as we traveled across the United States to study the measina of American Samoa. Thank you to: The Smithsonian Institution, Brooklyn Museum, American Museum of Natural History, Cooper Hewitt Museum, Winterthur Program at the University of Delaware, Harvard University, Yale University, Rhode Island School of Design, The Field Museum of Chicago, University of Oregon, Milwaukee Public Museum, and DeYoung Museum of San Francisco.

Thank you to the artists, conservators, advocates, and educators who took the time to speak with me about siapo and who contributed whole-heartedly to this book. Thank you to: Su'a Uilisone Fitiao,

Reggie Meredith Fitiao, Nicholas King, Talanoa Lagafuaina, Pua To-faeono, Christopher Philipp, Alyssa Rina, and Michele Austin-Dennehy.

Thank you to the siapo makers of yesterday, to women like Mary J. Pritchard, Kolone Leoso, Tui'uli Leoso, and all of the women who came before them. I've never met you, but I've seen the art that has sprung from your creative lineage here in American Samoa. Your influence knows no bounds.

Thank you to Su'a Uilisone Fitiao and Reggie Meredith Fitiao for your love and support, your expert knowledge, and your lifetime of dedication to this beautiful art form. I'm proud to be your daughter.

Thank you to my mom, Debbie Dowling, for filling my childhood with books and love. I'm constantly amazed by your strength and patience. Thank you to my brothers and sisters–Michael, Esme, Joe, and Faith–for your friendship and laughter and phone calls on tough days. Thank you to my grandparents, aunts, uncles, fathers, and other family members for your support. Thank you to the teachers who have inspired my writing over the years, with a special thanks to Dustin M. Hoffman. Thank you to my brilliant editor, Rachel Reeher, for helping ready this book for the readers. Thank you to my dear friends in American Samoa, the United States, and France–you have added so much joy to my life in countless ways.

Finally, thank you to the love of my life, my husband Fynn Peck. I'll never stop searching for the words that can express how much I love you.

About the Author

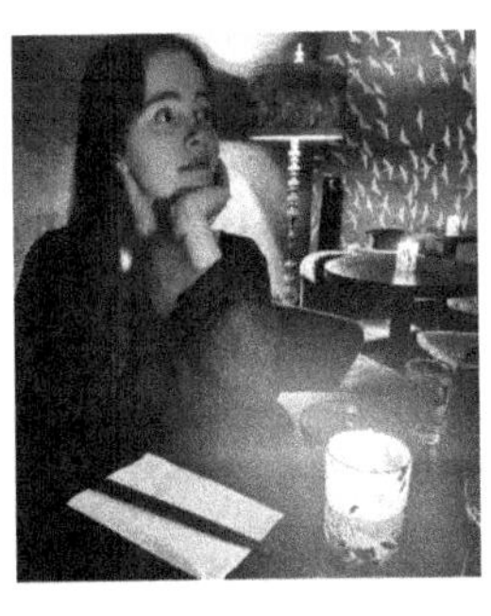

MARY ANNE PECK is a writer, educator, and workshop facilitator living in American Samoa. Originally from South Carolina, Mary earned her B.A. in English/Creative Writing from Winthrop University. After graduation, she moved to France and then to American Samoa, where she now lives with her husband in Taputimu. In 2020, Mary left full-time teaching to focus on her writing, working with clients such as Fa'asamoa Arts, the American Samoa Alliance Against Domestic and Sexual Violence, and others to create educational content, share life stories, and offer writing workshops for the community. Mary is currently pursuing her Master of Fine Arts in Fiction at the Warren Wilson College MFA Program for Writers. Mary's short stories have been published by *BULL Magazine*, *Back Patio Press*, *Epistemic Literary*, and *Taco Bell Quarterly*. Information about Mary's publications and workshops can be found at maryannepeck.com.

www.ingramcontent.com/pod-product-compliance
Lightning Source LLC
Chambersburg PA
CBHW050808260726

48660CB00004B/1309